Acknowledgements

The authors wish to acknowledge the support and encouragement they have received from OPL Spain, OPL France and OPL UK Ltd. and from NCC Blackwell Ltd. They particularly wish to thank the Spanish Government who helped to fund OPL Spain's initial involvement in *RISKMAN* by supporting the EUREKA initiative. Special thanks are also due to Anne Le Gall of OPL Toulouse whose knowledge of scheduling made this work possible.

A number of leading practitioners in the fields of risk and project management have also made valuable suggestions and comments, and the authors particularly wish to thank the following:

Professor Antonio de Amescua works at the Department of Engineering in the Carlos III University of Madrid. He is the Director of the Software Engineering Laboratory working in R&D projects in the areas of software testing, software development methodologies, software quality, software process maturity and risk management.

John Bartlett is a project management consultant with IBM UK Ltd., and a certificated member of the Association of Project Managers. He specialises in risk management techniques and has written and contributed to numerous papers on the subject.

Jacques Bertrand, after a 20 year career in project development and management with a major Belgian software house, has taken the *risk* of launching PSUtec, his own consultancy company in Belgium.

Paul Best worked in project management for a large defence manufacturer for 10 years. He has been a manager of design and is a Chartered Engineer. Now with Frazer-Nash Consultancy, he is deeply involved with project management and risk.

Graeme Clements is a civil engineer who started his career in Britain, rising quickly to contracts manager with a specialist subcontractor. He went on to major construction projects world-wide, most recently with a petrochemical company in the Arabian Gulf.

Bernard Curtis is a British Chartered Civil Engineer and Arbitrator, specialising in construction industry contracts, dispute resolution, and methodologies for better project management. He is an active researcher and lecturer on project risk management.

Geoff Fairall is an independent IT Management Consultant with over 30 years' project experience, specialising in the Banking and Financial sectors in Southern Africa.

Paulo de Gaetano is a member of IEEE and the Society for Computer Simulation. He has over 20 years' experience in projects, estimating and risk, both in his native Italy and several other European countries.

Andrew Greener is Technical Director of Westland Design Services Ltd. He has managed defence projects including an international collaborative NATO project, and was Programme Manager for the US Naval Airship Programme.

Steve Harcombe is the Technical Director of Advanced Software Engineering Ltd. A Chartered Engineer, he has been involved with real time systems development in the process industry, at British Steel, at RCA Corporation and the Serco Group.

Michael Hill is a Senior Lecturer in Project Management at the Civil Service College, England. He has over 15 years' Information Systems experience, gained working with the Royal Air Force, the Royal Navy, the British Army, the Royal Dockyards, CCTA, HM Treasury and other UK Government departments.

David Hillson is a Senior Consultant with HVR Consulting Services Ltd. and has wide experience in assessing risk for major UK and international defence projects. He is a member of the Association of Project Managers Special Interest Group on Risk.

Jean-Pierre Jullien is involved in risk management procurement for armament programmes in the French MoD. He has 5 years' experience in submarine weapons systems, integration and fire safety.

John A. Kiralfy is a Programme Manager with AT&T/NCR based in Dayton, Ohio, USA. He has been in Information Technology Programmes for over 15 years, with assignments in South Africa, the UK and the USA, and is currently implementing Project Management methodologies.

Eric Mahey has worked as both a Civil Servant and in Industry. He is a Charter Member of the International Society of Parametric Analysts, has chaired the Society for Cost Analysis and Forecasting, and sits on the International Electrotechnical Commission Working Groups responsible for Life-cycle Costing and Risk Analysis. He has developed a variety of computerised parametric and risk management models,

Christian Ritter gained his Ph.D. in statistics at the University of Wisconsin, USA. He is a researcher at the Centre for Operations Research and Econometrics at Universite Catholique de Louvain, Belgium, and a statistical consultant.

Jim Williams has over 20 years' experience in the telecommunications industry, with the past 10 years in a variety of project management roles. He is a member of the Association of Project Managers, the Institution of Electrical Engineers, and the British Psychological Society. He is particularly interested in people's perception of risk.

Disclaimer

Foreword

In the 1990s we are all facing a more challenging business environment than at any time in the past. Competition philosophy rules. Customer service expectations have never been higher. Global boundaries are disappearing. Mergers, acquisitions and cross-border joint ventures are creating giant companies with globally competitive ambitions. Speed of response is crucial. Unfamiliarity is a familiar problem. Major customers are demanding that multi-billion pound projects be delivered within demanding fixed-price budgets and tight timescales. To us in business, all of these factors lead to one thing: **Risk**. So we had better be able to manage risk if we want to stay in business into the next century.

Within the Systems and Services Division of British Aerospace Defence we have recognised the challenges of the 1990s marketplace and two years ago I was asked to put our risk management policies on a more formal basis. Since then my team has developed a strategic risk management methodology covering the total business life-cycle and addressing risks across functional boundaries. This methodology enables us both to manage the risks to the success of our businesses and projects, and to service the needs of our customers who require visibility of formal risk management. Our emphasis has leant heavily towards the active *management* of risk, rather than the mere identification and assessment of it, and is based on the four simple principles of:

- identifying for each business or project a detailed and explicit definition of what constitutes success, both to the customer and the company

- identifying all potential risks that pose threats to the achievement of each of the success factors, together with an assessment of their effect

- generating detailed mitigation strategies to counter each of the major threats to success

- having control mechanisms in place to ensure the mitigation strategies are indeed achieving their desired effect, allowing further refinements of the mitigation measures as necessary.

An important part of the risk management activity lies in harnessing the experience and knowledge of the entire management population in a project to anticipate and overcome risks. Hence successful risk management fundamentally depends on people, their knowledge, their energy and their creativity, rather than on computers and complex statistical simulations.

Software-based tools play an important part in risk *assessment*, but must, in our view, be seen in the context of the overall risk management process.

The *RISKMAN* methodology in this book presents a practical, hands-on approach to the management of risk that draws on our experience and is very much in line with our thinking. Properly applied, a formal risk management methodology should provide a focus on the key goals of the organisation and on overcoming the threats to their achievement. It should also result in an open culture that generates fact rather than opinion, clarity rather than smoke-and-mirrors, and pro-active control of risks at an early stage, rather than retrospective fire-fighting and the management of crisis. In turn, this cultural change should result in improved corporate performance, both in terms of meeting customers' expectations on time and within budget, and in delivering a sound financial performance to shareholders.

I commend the *RISKMAN* methodology to you as a practical approach to a subject that we all need to be familiar with in today's complex and competitive business environment. The views I have expressed are my own, and are not necessarily the views of British Aerospace.

Steve Marsh
October 1993

Steve Marsh is head of
Business Risk Management
in the Systems and Services Division
of British Aerospace Defence

Preface

About the EUREKA Project

The *RISKMAN* consortium was formed in late 1990 and approved in 1991 under the Eureka research programme, partly-funded by the governments of partners in the consortium. Its aim was to increase the professionalism with which project risk is managed by industry within the European Community.

Whilst a major target of the *RISKMAN* initiative was to provide improved computerised assistance for risk management in projects, it was clear that a methodology was needed as a prerequisite. Risk analysis techniques proliferate, together with books on the subject, but a general framework within which to apply them was conspicuous by its absence. Guidelines existed in a few specialised areas such as defence and information technology. However, no plans could be found to develop such a general framework outside these specialised areas.

December 1990	Creation of consortium
	Proposal submission
September 1991	First technical meeting: work starts
December 1991	*RISKMAN* authorised as Eureka
	project EU 530
June 1992	First draft of methodology
	Tool specification starts
	Methodology development starts
September 1992	Second draft of methodology
	Training materials
	Extensive methodology trials
December 1992	Methodology up-date
	Tool design starts
June 1993	First information seminar in UK
	Agreement to publish methodology
November 1993	First UK trial
January 1994	Launch of *RISKMAN* publications
Starting in 1994	*RISKMAN* manuals to be published
Starting in 1994	User groups to be set up

***RISKMAN* initiative milestones**

In the Spring of 1993, the OPL Group decided to publish the *RISKMAN* methodology. That decision has led to this introductory volume, which is the first in a set of publications that will detail the methodology and that are planned for release over the next twelve months.

OPL is an independent group of consultancy and training companies based in Europe, but also represented in North America and Australia.

It is one of several consultancies in the *RISKMAN* Consortium, and was selected to manage the development and documentation of the methodology because of its extensive knowledge and background in this area.

The future of *RISKMAN*

The *RISKMAN* methodology has been tested on a number of pilot projects with considerable success. It is now anticipated that organisations throughout Europe will increasingly adopt the methodology and become committed users, applying it throughout their organisations.

User groups are planned, and it is intended that these groups will participate in the ownership, control and development of the methodology in future years. The user groups will be independent, and membership will be open to all those applying the methodology or having interest in it (such as those considering adopting it, or others such as professional associations). This has been selected as the most effective way to guarantee the integrity of the methodology for the future.

BRAINWARE (Greece)
BULL (France)
CCC (Finland)
CR2A (France)
ELSYP (Greece)
OPL-TT (Spain)
SYSECA (France)
THOMSON CSF (France)
Members of the   ***RISKMAN* Consortium**

Copyright on this particular volume has been retained for the present by OPL who have provided the authors. Copyright on the *RISKMAN* manual set itself, due for publication in 1994, (see Appendix A) will eventually be vested in a design authority board which will be composed of the publisher, representatives of the original partners in the *RISKMAN* initiative, and representatives from user groups.

This mechanism has been established to provide for the continued use and development of the methodology beyond the time when the EUREKA project itself has come to an end. As a focus for this activity in future, an annual conference on project and risk management is envisaged, circulating around suitable European venues.[1]

Several members of the consortium are curently working on the development of a software tool which should be available during 1995.

---

[1] Readers interested in more information regarding *RISKMAN* activity and user groups are invited to contact one of the following:

Spain   Olivier Houri Tel. +34-1-571-7833   **France**   Jean-Marc Morin Tel. +33-6180-9140
UK   Ned Robins   Tel. +44-737-370439   **Belgium** Luc Griffet   Tel. +32-2-374-6468

Authors

Eric Bruce Carter

In the course of an extensive career, Bruce Carter worked on the installation and commissioning of the Ballistic Missile Early Warning Station and on the UK Polaris Weapon System installation. He moved on to maritime consultancy and then joined British Aerospace in the Naval Systems Management Group and has worked on the development and production of a strategic risk management policy. He now consults in risk with OPL.

Tony Hancock

Tony Hancock is a senior consultant with OPL UK. After becoming involved with warship refitting projects in the Navy, he spent some years lecturing at the Royal Military College of Science (Shrivenham). He has since held senior positions in industry and more recently in consulting activities, becoming heavily involved with the development of computerised project support systems, and the associated technology transfer into industry.

Jean-Marc Morin

Jean-Marc Morin is the Vice President of OPL, and is in charge of research projects within the OPL Group. He is a specialist in systems engineering, and leads high level consultancy operations. Following a degree in computer science he worked in real-time systems at IGL, and then joined Aerospatiale to work on MIS projects. He holds the French equivalent of Chartered Engineer status as an information systems engineer.

M J Robins

Ned Robins is a managing consultant with OPL UK, and has considerable industrial experience as a manager and executive. He regularly contributes to degree courses at a number of UK universities, and has been consulting and lecturing for the past decade in specialist aspects of project management.

Contents

1
Background to *RISKMAN*

In this chapter, we will examine the purpose of the *RISKMAN* methodology. We will explain what *RISKMAN* is, how it works, and also what are its limits.

We will explain what we mean by a methodology and what you can expect to gain from it, but also what its limitations are and what commitments you will be undertaking if you decide to adopt it.

What the *RISKMAN* team have found is that a more successful approach to the management of project risk is likely to require a deep-seated change within management. So deep-seated in fact that it may, in some instances, be called a culture change — one which involves re-education at all levels right up to the top of the organisation. Without a cultural change, staff will continue to be wary about sharing their understanding of the risks that the organisation is taking. Only once such change is implemented will they be ready to start to quantify risk and communicate their knowledge for the benefit of the company, instead of concealing contingencies in their estimates and failing to alert management to the deterioration in project status.

The implications of *RISKMAN* are clearly far-reaching, and by the end of this chapter, the reader will realise why it has been decided to publish the methodology in three-manual set. We will conclude by explaining what we hope to achieve in this first introductory paperback, and how this volume has been assembled and can be used.

1.1 Purpose of *RISKMAN*

The purpose of the *RISKMAN* methodology is to provide a general framework for professional project risk analysis and control, and guidance for its implementation. Since projects vary so much in size and scope, their requirements with regard to risk management techniques also vary. The methodology has therefore been deliberately constructed to facilitate flexibility. It is not intended to be rigid or prescriptive. Neither is it intended to constitute a standard as such, though its layered approach with three levels could also be used to provide guidance for categorising risk management activity for audit assessments.

The methodology is intended to achieve six specific aims, listed in Figure 1.1. These can be summarised within an overall aim of providing a sound basis for effective communication about methods used by project participants to manage risk. The benefits of effectively managing the risks accrue to all parties, including: project sponsor (funder); customer (user); prime contractor; subcontractor; project team members and the project manager. This is likely to be increasingly important with the proliferation of European collaborative projects, where the need for a consistent and documented approach to project risk management has become imperative.

- **To increase professional capability in the taking of risks in project environments.**

- **To promote general understanding of risk and probabilistic theory amongst management and staff at all levels.**

- **To provide general principles for effective risk management.**

- **To provide specific guidance on a framework within which project risk can be effectively managed.**

- **To clarify terminology which may form a sound basis for effective communication about risk.**

- **To examine, clarify, assess and provide guidance on the methods and techniques available for risk analysis and management.**

Figure 1.1 Specific aims of the methodology

It should be noted that the purpose of *RISKMAN* is not to avoid or remove risk, but rather to enable and encourage project participants to selectively and deliberately take the risks that they choose, on terms that are known and acceptable. The professional approach to risk is to seek to optimise and control risk-taking in order to acquire maximum potential benefit, whilst facing a limited and controlled exposure to suffering harm or loss.

The methodology is not intended to constitute a technique or collection of techniques which managements may opt to apply to this project or that, but not to the other. Whilst it could be used that way, it embodies a philosophy which, if fully embraced, permanently changes the way that all your projects will be managed.

If an organisation adopts *RISKMAN*, this will mean embedding its principles into its project management procedures and applying it across the board. Thereafter, individual projects within the organisation may be identified as requiring only a basic level of risk management, or an intermediate or a comprehensive level. Whilst different projects may be managed using different mixes of the range of risk management techniques, they will all be managed within the *RISKMAN* methodology.

1.2 Why a methodology?

We should explain why we have chosen to call *RISKMAN* a methodology, and what we mean by that term.   It is necessary to consider the differences between a methodology and a philosophy, a method, a set of procedures, a collection of techniques, and a standard.

There is a consistent philosophy concerning the management of uncertainty in projects that is embodied within *RISKMAN*, and which underpins every aspect of it. This philosophy teaches that:

- Risk, or uncertainty, is an integral, inevitable and important feature of all project scenarios, and one which has not been given sufficient attention since the advent of critical path analysis in the 1960s;

- Risk should be respected, but not feared. It should be handled systematically and carefully;

- The pro-active control of significant risks and threats to the achievement of project objectives is so important, that it should be the highest priority for the project manager;

- When managed professionally, risk-taking can provide real opportunities to maximise potential benefits for all concerned, and yield higher profit and/or benefit returns than low-risk enterprises;

- If risk is to be managed professionally, an analytical and quantitative approach is essential, combined with a real understanding of probability and uncertainty theory;

- The mathematical approach is essential for the evaluation of risk, but alone it is impotent. People must be involved if risk is to be controlled and risk opportunities exploited. The human approach must run hand in hand with the mathematical approach;

- Since the project manager must bring in all project deliverables within budgeted time and cost, that budget should include a contingency budget sufficient to address all uncertainties (i.e. all risk) as best can be forecast. This also means that the contingency should be justified **explicitly** in advance of commitment to the budget;

- Advance justification of risk contingency will encourage honesty in the estimating process and the acceptance of progressive management combining openness with responsibility;

- Risks must be owned by individuals. Risk causes must also be owned, monitored and mitigated. Early action is usually lower in cost and more effective than management by crisis.

Whilst there is a clear and consistent philosophy and theoretical basis for *RISKMAN*, it is very definitely not just a philosophy. *RISKMAN* is intended to be primarily practical rather than theoretical and to be used to promote action. It contains much more than a philosophy.

The larger part of *RISKMAN* is intended to provide advice on how to **do** risk management. The theory is important, but the methods used to apply that theory are more important. There have been many volumes published about risk, particularly about risk analysis, but it is very difficult to find any text which tells the reader how to actually perform the job of managing risk.

It has been argued that there are at least three methods for managing risk outlined in *RISKMAN*. The authors prefer to describe *RISKMAN* as one method with guidance on three levels of application of that method, and flexibility to *mix and match* from any or all of those three levels. Associated with the use of *RISKMAN* is the application of selections from a large range of techniques. The project environment is diverse enough for a rigid method to be inadequate. *RISKMAN* provides guidance to users on the tailoring of the methodology for their own environment, whether that be, for example, pharmaceutical research, large multinational collaborative development projects, or repetitive build projects in a jobbing shop or on a construction site. In the same way that *RISKMAN* is more than a philosophy, it is equally more than a method or a set of procedures.

With regard to techniques suitable for risk management, they abound. Some have been developed specifically for risk management, whilst many others may be readily applied to risk management, even though they were not designed with risk management specifically in mind. There is such a wealth of information here, that a complete manual is planned to cover this subject. However, far from being a collection of techniques, *RISKMAN* is designed to help the project manager decide which techniques are relevant to his current problems and how to apply them. In other words, the authors believe that advice on which ones to **avoid** is as important as guidance on how to use the ones that are suitable.

Whenever consultants and academics become interested in a subject like risk, there is a danger of becoming swamped by techniques. Current textbooks and software offerings for risk management are in danger of discouraging interested project managers from getting involved. This is because of their heavy reliance on relatively obscure statistical theory, and an emphasis on accurate processing of inaccurate data rather than providing assistance to accurately identify and quantify the right risks in the first place. Practising project professionals are looking for practical advice on simple steps to take in moving forward. The *RISKMAN* publications may contain many words about techniques, but again, it has to be more than a mere collection of techniques.

We may summarise this discussion so far by saying that this methodology:

- is based on a consistent philosophy;
- provides three levels of application of one method;
- attempts to provide guidance on techniques to call upon in any particular circumstance;
- focuses attention on how to do it rather than why it should be done;
- recognises that there is a need for tailoring in any one application, and provides advice on that tailoring;
- is as much an approach to the management of projects based on uncertainty, as a method for managing uncertainty in project environments;
- attempts to provide guidance on how to modify project management procedures, but is much more than a mere set of procedures.

So it is clear why *RISKMAN* could not be called a philosophy, a method, a single set of procedures or a collection of techniques. This is why the *RISKMAN* Team settled on the choice of the term *methodology*. However, this still leaves the issue of *standards* to be addressed.

The *RISKMAN* Team have attempted to encapsulate *best practice* in project risk management. Therefore it is reasonable to hope that *RISKMAN* may prove useful at some point in the future to anybody who sets out to establish a standard for risk management. However, *RISKMAN* has not been developed thus far with any intention of being used as a standard in itself. The *RISKMAN* Team have not presumed to undertake such a task, and indeed there is pressure for the International Standards Organisation to consider such a standard. Audit of risk management activity is an inevitable part of implementing *RISKMAN*, but its objective has not been to certificate any particular level of competence in risk management, but rather to help in improving that competence level.

1.3 Implications of *RISKMAN*

The full implementation of the *RISKMAN* methodology in the form of *risk-driven project management* amounts to a significant change in emphasis in the discipline of project management. This does not mean abandoning or superseding the rules established as current wisdom. Indeed, it is essential to stick to established rules in order to make the risk-driven approach work. However, conventional wisdom centres on developing the main plan and focusing attention on trying to adhere to that plan. Risk management starts when one realises that the plan itself is full of uncertainty. The real project professional pays most attention to the plan in order to identify and control those things that can prevent achievement of the plan, or can go wrong within it. He does not attempt the impossible task of trying to adhere slavishly to the plan, rather he tries to pro-actively control any threats to achievement of project objectives.

The assumption made by most people trying to implement what is accepted as sound project management is that: *the plan is what you are actually going to do.* This is not really the case in a project environment (as explained in Section 2.3.1). The real reasons that a plan is so important are:

1.   It is the basis for decision-making and adjustments throughout the project's implementation phase.

2.   Planning provides the greatest likelihood that the most efficient path will be taken through the project.

3.   The project plan is helpful in identifying the detail of the risks to the project.

So the risk-driven approach depends upon the prior establishment of current wisdom or current best practice. It may be argued that the risk-driven approach is the logical next step in the evolution of formal project management methods and techniques. We will explain the context of the risk-driven approach within the evolution of project management thinking in Section 2.3. The conclusion of this discussion must be that implementing *RISKMAN* has major implications for the practice of project management itself. The risk-driven approach involves a major change in emphasis towards the pro-active management of uncertainty as the key to success in project management.

RISKMAN will be seen as new by many readers. Indeed the authors believe that the collation of a systematic and complete approach to risk is new. There are also a number of new elements developed within *RISKMAN*. However, it is mainly the collation that is new, rather than the elements that have been collated. The authors have started from the premise that *RISKMAN* represents a deliberate move to re-establish and recognise what has always been good project management practice, but to do so in a structured and organised manner so that good project management will be made better and more effective in relation to uncertainty.

1.4 The need for culture change

Western civilisation has become increasingly steeped in a deterministic view of the world over many centuries as science has achieved supremacy over mysticism. Traditional science teaches us that we can be sure of a specific outcome if we control the inputs to a given reaction or activity. Whilst Einstein's Theory of Relativity is now 80 years old, and whilst modern scientists currently focus on theories of chaos, ordinary mortals are yet to be heavily influenced by this change in thinking. This means that individuals at all levels in the business world have great difficulty in living with the concept of uncertainty.

When a senior manager asks a project manager what the probability is of achieving target schedule and profitability, the question seems to indicate that he understands all about uncertainty. Indeed, he would be offended if you challenged him on that understanding because he does know that nothing is certain in the project world. On the other hand, action speaks louder than words, and it is clear from observation of a wide range of organisations that what they expect from the project manager is nothing less than delivery on target regardless of the problems. This is not an unrealistic expectation from people who have been educated in a deterministic system founded on the science of Dalton and Newton, especially in a Protestant society where risk is little short of an emotional dirty word, due to its close associations with gambling and gaming.[2]

We are not suggesting here that senior management is incapable of understanding probability theory, but rather that they are not used to having risk presented to them in a meaningful way. We are prepared to suggest, however, that a communications gap has developed between disciplines, and particularly between engineering and both the financial function and senior management. Mistrust has built up gradually over an extensive period, at least over a century and a half since the days of Brunel. Experienced engineers hide contingency allowance in all their estimates because they know that senior management will enter into an internal negotiation to reduce *costs* before submitting a bid in order to have the most competitive price and win

---

[2]See: *Religion and the Rise of Capitalism*, R H Tawney, Pelican, 1938, and/or *The Protestant Ethic and the Spirit of Capitalism*, Max Weber, Unwin Univ. Books, 1930

the business. Of course senior management cannot really reduce costs at this stage. What that statement means is that they are going to push down the *estimates*. So the first estimates submitted will not be the engineers' genuine best guesses, but are the opening gambits for the forthcoming battle!

Project professionals have always had a clear understanding of risk even though they may not be steeped in probability theory, and may have difficulty quantifying and presenting that understanding. The very word *estimate* means: *I have some idea about what this should cost, but there is a degree of uncertainty about the number.* However, engineers and development staff do not believe that senior management or the financial function will permit them to have as much reserve for contingency action as they really do need. This is entirely justified. Over the years, it has been found that experienced engineers always have some more contingency up their sleeves. If pushed hard enough, they will often reduce estimates still further and yet still appear to complete the job on target. What non-engineers do not realise is that this is commonly achieved by booking time to another job where some contingency reserve was hidden, or where there was a positive risk occurrence. This may be regarded as blatant dishonesty by the accounts department, but it protects the professional standing of the engineer, diverting what is often unjustified criticism of the original estimates which was caused by 'the system' of having to negotiate the allowed target rather than calculating it.

Let us clarify this point with a real-life example:

> A project consultant was recently invited to re-train engineering teams who, it was said, had *forgotten* how to estimate! Engineers do not forget how to estimate! The truth is that the management involved had failed to understand their current position. The company concerned is in an over-competitive, shrinking market. In response, management had shed many of their experienced people in re-organisations and cut-backs, whilst tightening estimates on everything, and worse still, imposing blanket reductions on the costings across whole projects.

> A case put forward in their boardroom three years ago was: we are in danger of not winning this bid unless we take 10% off the price, and we will not be able to grow this contract with lots of variation orders (procurement executives got wise to that one in 1985). Also we have to predict an increased profit level at next week's shareholder's meeting to bolster the share price. We know that those overcautious engineers always have lots of contingency built in to their estimates. They are a lazy lot anyway, and it is time we merged the design function with the new subsidiary which we acquired last year and has those nice offices on the South Coast. That will give us the chance to get rid of some dead wood, bring in new blood, improve engineering efficiency and cut costs. Strategy on this one has to be to cut all the estimates by 20%, put target

contribution back up to normal and indeed we can increase it by 4%, and that will still leave us a hidden contingency of 2% in case things go wrong! Better still, if we land the job we will spend that 2% on a recruitment campaign to bring in some really enthusiastic young project managers, and all our problems will be solved!

Unfortunately we are now three years down the line and the birds have come home to roost. The result is that the consultant is being called into a design office where morale is at an all time low. Most of the senior engineers who signed off the estimates three years ago have taken early retirement. Any remaining experienced engineers who were with the company then, remember what the original estimates were. They have zero commitment to these new estimates which they consider unachievable. They also appreciate that the new CAD system, which was brought in to *improve design efficiency by 30%* requires an eight month learning curve before it brings any benefits, and current work packages must be completed before then. In any case the 30% calculation for CAD was based on a redesign level of 40%, mostly due to variation orders, but since the TQM system is focusing attention on getting things right first time, and the customer is refusing to contemplate any variations, there may be no benefits to be had. The biggest problem of all is that there is simply no work in the department with hidden contingency reserve, so there is nowhere to hide over-plan hours.

Suddenly, all design work is costing more than it should, and the whole function seems to be out of control. This has never happened before. It appears to management that engineering have now forgotten how to do an estimate! We had better call in an outside expert to retrain them to do an estimate properly!

Unfortunately in this scenario it seems that the management concerned have missed the point. Far from getting to grips with the problem, they are about to exacerbate it further. Calling in the outside consultant is only liable to indicate that they do not consider their engineers to be professionally capable, but those engineers are not actually to blame for the current impossible costings anyway. Management regard the design function as responsible for all the company's current problems, whilst this is the complete opposite of the truth. It is really the management itself which has created the problem, therefore what they should really ask the consultant to do is resolve the problems of the management.

This may be an extreme case, but the breakdown of communication which really caused the problem is actually fairly typical of a wide range of organisations. What is needed is a complete change in management style, a culture change, throughout the project world, from the top to the bottom.

This is an extensive demand to make. It has to start with re-education at the top of the organisation, not near the bottom. It requires a change of attitude to management of risks at the top, and a commitment to drive that change down through every level to the bottom. The scale of the problem should not be underestimated. It will be very difficult to break the vicious circle. Realistic estimates are only going to be provided when people are confident that they will not be subject to cuts. Equally, if management unilaterally starts accepting estimates as submitted, the resultant prices will be too high for them to get any more business. This process can be eased by making the risk provisions explicit with justifying documentation, but it will be a mistake to think that the job will be easy.

There is a grave temptation when a manager discovers *RISKMAN* to rush into changing company procedures and training people to execute the process, without giving thought to changing attitudes. Whilst this is motivated by a genuine desire to improve efficiency, it could be a mistake similar to that made by the management in the previous example which is to treat the symptom, not the cause. In many cases there can be great benefit in commissioning a *formal assessment audit* prior to implementing *RISKMAN*, to evaluate the extent of the need for culture change in the organisation, and the best means of introducing it. When the culture change problem is under control, implementing risk management procedures, whilst still difficult, will be relatively easy in comparison, and should be successful.

1.5 Risk management current practice

1.5.1 Background

It is very difficult to generalise about the current situation with regard to risk management. There is a great variation between different industries and between operators within those industries. Each observer sees a limited view which may be individually accurate, but not representative of the overall picture. The problem is exacerbated by the fact that there are a few very influential procurement bodies who are keen to encourage increased professionalism in risk management. This is clearly desirable, but it has a sad side-effect. In order to impress these procurement bodies and to win business, suppliers go to some lengths to show that they have made massive steps in the right direction, when in fact they have made little or no real progress. The result is that some people really believe that the state of the art is much more advanced than is borne out by the truth.

The analytic approach to project risk management was given a major boost in the 1980s in the oil industry. This was driven by a desire to solve scheduling problems against tight delivery targets for the exploitation of North Sea oil despite very uncertain and dangerous weather conditions. Since then the reins

□ **Tunnel Vision Strategy**
We will try this way
Succeed 100% or fail 100%

□ **Benefactor Strategy**
Whatever it costs we will do it

□ **Gilding the Lily Strategy**
Over-specifying the problem

□ **Octopus Strategy:**
Nobody takes a decision
Decision depends on mood of leader
Lack of realism

□ **Shoot the Messenger Strategy**
This is an excellence company.
If someone exposes an error we sack him.

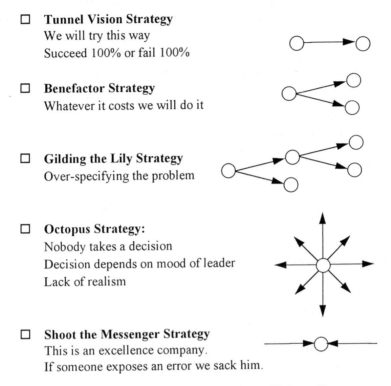

Figure 1.2 Strategies typically uncovered by OPL audits

have been largely taken up in the defence arena with pressure on defence
contractors to manage risk, particularly in Britain and the USA. Here, too, the
analytic techniques are often focused on handling schedule problems, but
increasingly and inevitably, the emphasis has come around to a higher
emphasis on cost risk rather than schedule risk. There are other isolated
pockets where advances have been made in areas like IT and utilities, but
these are exceptions rather than the rule. This history of interest in risk
management has resulted in a situation where there is a clear picture
established in a few isolated areas of how managements want to proceed. A
philosophy has been developed, an approach established and procedures laid
down. Pilot projects have been selected and the procedures are starting to be
applied and tested. However, even here, it is generally true to say that this
approach to project risk has not been implemented across the board. In most
areas it is seen as new, and still developing. There is a generally recognised
need for some degree of standardisation of approach, and this has been a
major contributor to the motivation for publication of *RISKMAN*. However, a
degree of flexibility must be provided to enable the approach to evolve
reflecting any further change that may occur.

Audits have found that even high technology companies who are considered to be at the forefront with regard to management techniques and who certainly consider themselves to be so, are generally sadly lacking when it comes to professional risk management.   Figure 1.2 illustrates typical strategies frequently uncovered in risk management audits carried out by OPL.

Mention needs to be made of other areas where there have been significant developments over the past few years. Major disasters, particularly in the oil, nuclear and chemicals spheres, have stimulated attention on risk reduction to protect the environment and human safety. A related, but distinct, area is that of product reliability and maintainability in which much work has been done. The third major area is that of disaster recovery. Particularly in the IT sector and again in oil and gas, a whole new industry has grown up around coping with the aftermath after major catastrophes have occurred.

Whilst there has not been the same amount of change recently in the more traditional areas of insurance and investment analysis, these also need to be taken into account in any complete description of the state of the art. A project risk management methodology such as that described in *RISKMAN* is likely to be thought of as a new concept by professionals in these areas, and whilst one hopes that they will applaud the development, they are likely to find much material which they consider strange, even though some of the tools and techniques will already be familiar to them.

RISKMAN attempts to pull all these various areas of development together into a homogeneous whole, but seen very specifically from the viewpoint of the project manager.

1.5.2 Current initiatives for standardisation

As mentioned earlier, standardisation is considered desirable, and a number of bodies have made moves in this direction. A Norwegian standard for risk analysis already exists, and an international standard is currently under discussion, though at present both are heavily focused toward safety, reliability and related risk. The UK Ministry of Defence has published guidelines on risk[3], and the CCTA[4] are in the process of publishing quite detailed guidelines for project risk. The CCTA have already published a methodology called CRAMM (CCTA Risk Analysis and Management Method[5]), but this is mostly concerned with data security and is very much aimed at information technology development. The Engineering Council in

---

[3]British MoD Risk Guidelines, published Jan 1992 and Jun 1993, ref D/DPP(PM)/2/1/12

[4]CCTA is a British government agency, once called the Central Computing and Telecommunications Agency, but now officially called simply the CCTA.

[5]Published by CCTA in 1988.

Britain has published a ten point Risk Code of Practice for its members, but this tends to focus on safety issues. The UK Association of Project Managers has also produced a small booklet on risk analysis which it distributes freely. Despite all these various initiatives, the *RISKMAN* team could not find any body that has published or intends to publish a comprehensive methodology as such. Hence the decision to publish *RISKMAN*.

1.5.3 Relationship of *RISKMAN* to other initiatives

A deliberate effort has been made to ensure that *RISKMAN* is compatible with other initiatives as far as possible. A central objective of *RISKMAN* has been to embody currently-targeted best practice, pulling it together and building on it rather than launching off in new directions.

1.5.4 Compatibility with standards

RISKMAN is intended to be compatible with these standards:

Quality: ISO9000, BS5750, TickIT
Project Management: PRINCE, C/SCSC, MoD & CCTA Guidelines.

1.6 Structure of this introductory volume

Having explained the background to the development of *RISKMAN* in the Foreword and Chapter 1, we will proceed in Chapter 2 to establish the context in which *RISKMAN* should reside. We will look at some of the theory and background of uncertainty in project management, and how all this fits into the business process.

In Chapter 3 we will explain some of the theoretical background to *RISKMAN* thinking.

In Chapter 4 we will look at the operation of the risk management process which cycles continually throughout the project life-cycle and how to document, control and use it to best advantage.

In Chapter 5 we will look at risk-driven project management, and how a constructive effort to manage uncertainty changes and completes the management disciplines already applied in project situations.

In the final two chapters we will look at the process of implementing *RISKMAN*, some of the difficulties that may be experienced, and the benefits that should result.

We have preceded each chapter with a short section introducing the chapter itself. The structure of the book as described can be expanded by simply reading the first section of each chapter.

2
Introduction to
Project Risk Management

In this chapter we take an introductory look at the nature of risk and its inter-relationship with projects. We will assert that project management consists only of project administration, i.e. planning and doing the things that are intended, and risk management, i.e. coping with uncertainty and all those things that do not go as intended. This leads directly to the conclusion that implementing the *RISKMAN* methodology does not mean developing good risk management procedures as a separate activity in its own right, rather that it involves changing the procedures for project-management itself. The significance for the management process of classifying risks will be outlined.

We will also seek to understand why risk has caused such problems in the past to managements who are responsible for project activities.

Creating a desire amongst staff to participate in pro-active risk management is not in itself enough to ensure success. So we will look a little deeper at some of the problems that are commonly encountered when people do start trying to identify, quantify and effectively report on project risk. Much work has been done in this area, and the *RISKMAN* team have deliberately tried to document what is recognised to be desired *best-practice* rather than setting out to design a new, untried (and therefore high risk) approach.

We will provide a short history of project management thinking, showing where risk fits in, and perhaps explaining why it has had so little attention over the last forty years.

We have already asserted that a deep-seated change is needed in many companies, so we will conclude by outlining the requirements that must be satisfied to achieve this cultural change. These requirements are the key factors that the *RISKMAN* team have set out to satisfy both in the methodology, and in their guidance on its implementation.

2.1 The risk concept

2.1.1 The simplicity of risk

Project risk is a complex issue which has many facets. Risk itself is a simple matter, though one that is poorly understood and often feared. Fundamentally a risk is composed of a cause about which there may be some uncertainty and an effect or impact about which there may also be some uncertainty.

Risk is variously defined in dictionaries, with words along the lines of: *the possibility of suffering harm or loss, or exposure to this.* The dictionary definition usually focuses on the unpleasant side of risk, and yet risk is potentially very profitable. Whereas investors expect low yields from gilt-edged securities, they often seek venture capital opportunities which have the potential for high returns enabling them to achieve a balanced investment portfolio. Risk management is potentially a positive opportunity to increase profitability. Risks are not all bad, and it is not uncommon to deliberately take a risk which potentially has a significant desirable outcome, as any lottery ticket holder will tell you.

Rather than quoting dictionaries in an attempt to understand exactly what is meant by risk we will do better to seek the common denominator in all definitions and say simply that *a risk involves uncertainty and has an impact.* Both the uncertainty and the impact are capable of quantification, and this permits a numeric definition much quoted in statistical treatises on risk which may use varying terminology, but basically runs as follows:

risk exposure[6] = *impact value* x *probability of occurrence*

This theory seems, and indeed is, simplistic in approach but is completely valid. However, applying it in project situations is by no means simple. If we were able to quantify the values of all the risks one had to face, the above theory would prove invaluable, but that is most unlikely to be the case in practice. Beware the theorists who ignore the difficulty of quantifying risk and the complexities involved in managing risk in the real-life situations faced by project managers. In reality, the main concern, if the risk occurs, is its full effect on costs, timescale and performance rather than its risk exposure value; and if it has not occurred, then whether it is still likely to occur in the future.

The most important aspects of a risk from a management point of view are its causes. Only by influencing the causes can the risk be pro-actively managed.

---

[6]An exposure can be valued negatively or positively. The beneficial (or positive) alternative is usually not included in the statistical treatises, but is necessary in view of the comments above on desirable risks.

You may note that causes are ignored in the sample definition above. Knowing a risk exposure value is only useful in analysing how important it is to manage that risk. It is not helpful in managing the risk actively.

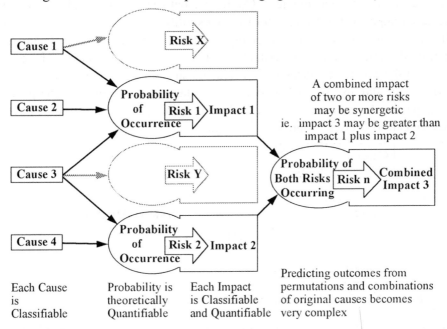

Figure 2.1 Exposure to risk

Unfortunately much confusion arises because common usage of risk terms is very loose. When people from different environments talk about risk, they are liable to be talking about different things. Environmentalists, health and safety professionals, and even many technical professionals and engineers assume that risk management is about preventing disasters like oil spillages or nuclear explosions or threats to human life. Information technology professionals assume that it is about data and system security and disaster recovery. Investment analysts believe that it is about stocks and shares. Insurance professionals believe that it is about the premium they should charge. The bank manager thinks it is about the risk in letting you have an overdraft. The marketing professional thinks it is about whether he can get customers for his newest product line. We must make very clear what *RISKMAN* is about. *RISKMAN* is concerned with **all** project risks. These may be technical risks, schedule risks, cost risks, and indeed almost any of the risks mentioned above. They may not all be the responsibility of the Project Manager, but they may all impinge on his project, and he must ensure that they are all managed properly by someone.

2.1.2 The complexity of risk

One risk impact may have several causes, and one cause may lead to several risks, each having one impact. Confusion between causes and effects can create a danger to the allocation of responsibility for risks. It is important to allocate responsibility and "ownership" quite clearly for each significant risk identified. The owner of the risk should be closest to the impact. There can be several owners of causes with whom he/she must maintain close liaison, and who should also be clearly identified. They must all report to the project manager for the execution of their risk responsibility who in turn must have a mechanism to exercise control in this regard.

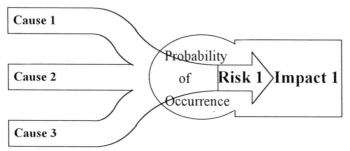

Figure 2.2   Complexity due to confusing causes with effects

In many cases the *relationship* between a cause and an impact may well be fairly certain and reasonably predictable. However, the cause and the impact themselves are going to have elements of uncertainty. In particular, estimates of the probability of occurrence are unlikely to be accurate, and there are no means of testing their accuracy. Let us illustrate this last statement with an example.

> Take a simple and unusually predictable risk - the rolling of six-sided dice. In this case we know that the likelihood of a particular number, say a 3, turning up is one in six. This we can calculate because of the physical characteristics of the circumstances. However, each time the die is cast, either a 3 turns up, or it does not. In either case that does not confirm that we had the probability calculation correct. We do know that if the die is cast sixty times we can expect 3 to turn up ten times on average. However if we do so, and 3 turns up only once, that proves nothing. If it turns up twenty times, that proves nothing. Even if it does turn up ten times on this occasion it proves nothing, as every throw is an independent event.

Translated to the project world, things are different in one key respect: whereas we can roll the dice many times to gain a statistical insight into the likelihood of the outcome, every real project is not only independent, but very different in character. This means that we can never prove whether our risk estimating and provisioning was justified or inadequate. When an uncertain event does occur it ceases to be a risk, it has become a fact. We now know what the impact really is, and only now will we be able to say if our risk provisioning was actually adequate to cover this occurrence. This however proves nothing about the accuracy of any forecast we may have made of the probability that the risk would occur in the first place, nor whether other risk occurrences will subsequently make further demands on what is left of our risk provisioning.

The situation is further complicated by the fact that neither the impact nor the likelihood of occurrence are going to be straightforward values in real project situations. They are much more likely to have a range of potential values best described by a distribution curve (not necessarily a normal distribution, and often a skewed one). The single risk that seemed so simple in theory, turns out in practice to be a complex interaction of the two variables. The reality of life for one project is that there are always many risks which will interact in different ways dependent not only on whether they happen, but on the order in which they happen and when. Rigorous modelling of risk is difficult; this is not because the theory is inaccurate or incomplete, but rather because of the initial uncertainty in predicting the values, and the way in which the world works. Modelling can, however, enable the uncertainties to be aggregated into a more meaningful whole, and this can still be useful to the project manager.

2.1.3 The dilemma of risk management

Does then the complexity of risk mean that it cannot be managed? To manage something is to control it. Control is a strong word with very deterministic connotations. In the nebulous and probabilistic sphere of risk taking, the best that a management can realistically attempt is to correctly foresee potential problems and influence them to minimise harm and maximise benefit.

There is, in fact, much that can be done. The first rule of risk management is to start working on the risks at the earliest possible opportunity. That is usually when the greatest impression can be made for the lowest cost.

There are two main opportunities:

- to reduce unfavourable impacts (or increase favourable ones);
- to work on the causes which will reduce the likelihood of occurrence (or instead increase it, if the impact is favourable).

This might seem a simple and basic approach in so complex a world as we have described, but it is the simple approach which is usually most effective in such circumstances. The objective is to try to optimise risks pro-actively, but one will often never know if action was really necessary.

The *RISKMAN* Methodology seeks to provide a simple structured approach for the effective management of risk. The statistical analysis approach is not dismissed within *RISKMAN:* at the most exhaustive level, considerable use is made of this approach within the Methodology. However, the *RISKMAN* Team concluded unanimously that the three most important contributions to improving project risk management are:

- to move risk management up to the top of the agenda within the project management sphere;

- to provide a structured approach to identifying and prioritising the **right** risks; and

- to ensure that positive action is taken by the individual who is best placed to manage and control any risk.

Note that emphasis is not on getting accurate estimates of probability for statistically valid processing of correct risk data - that may on many occasions be impossible anyway. The emphasis is on ensuring that one has correctly identified the most important risks in the first place, and that one has a strategy in place to manage the situation. This means understanding each risk thoroughly in terms of who can influence it and how.

Manageable and unmanageable risks all have to be subjected to the management process. A risk is *unmanageable* when one cannot affect either its causes or its impact cost and neither can one influence its likelihood of occurrence. The risk may be impossible to control, yet you may still decide to take it. If you do take such a risk, you will still have to monitor it and ensure that contingency reserves remain adequate to cope should its risk status change. In this sense, even unmanageable risks have to be managed.

2.1.4 Risk-driven project management

Projects belong at the one-off end of the *Spectrum of Production and Operations Environments*[7]. This means that high flexibility and uncertainty, i.e. risk, are intrinsic to projects. Indeed it is this very uncertainty which makes project management difficult but also exciting and worth doing. The task of project management in fact only consists of two types of work:

- Getting all the things in the plan done - i.e. the administration;

- Handling all the things that go wrong - i.e. managing the risks.

---

[7]As described in many operations management texts, but first discussed and most fully developed by Terry Hill in *Production and Operations Management,* published by Prentice/Hall International in 1983 - see Figure 6.2.

Whilst the first of these activities is essential to the smooth running of the programme, it is the second of these which is important if the project is to be successful. Many project professionals have made a habit of hiding (or ignoring) the risks faced in their project so that others will not get worried and interfere. Nevertheless, they do have the skill and experience to manage the risks, provided they are asked to do so in the right environment. This realisation has caused the *RISKMAN* team to coin the phrase **Risk-driven project management** in an attempt to move risk up to the top of the agenda.

This leads directly to the conclusion that implementing the *RISKMAN* Methodology does not mean developing good risk management procedures as a separate activity in its own right, rather that it involves incorporating good risk management within the procedures for project management itself. The *RISKMAN* initiative will result in a set of manuals, not to go on the shelf, but to be used to extend and update your existing project management procedures. Risk must become accepted as a normal part, indeed the primary aspect, of the project management task and be fully integrated into the process. While the first item on the agenda of each project review is the progress to date, the very next item must be to review risk developments since the last meeting.

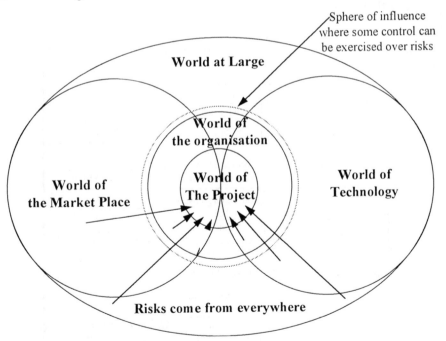

Figure 2.3 The project world

2.1.5 Understanding risk in projects

The project world exists within the environment created by the organisation. The organisation lives within several worlds which include the world of the market place, and the world of the technology which the company uses. All these live within the politico-economic world and the world at large. As indicated in Figure 2.3, all these worlds contribute to risk in the project.

All the risks have to be managed. During the conception phase of a project, many strategic, commercial and marketing decisions have to be made by senior management. When the project manager takes the reins, much of the risk is already embedded. Some of that risk is more manageable by him, and some is less. Beyond this point in the project life-cycle, he should have much control over the extent to which risk is taken. However, he is still likely to have only limited control over much of that risk.

Whenever a risk is more effectively influenced or controlled by someone else in the project world (other than the project manager himself), that person should be identified and given ownership of the risk. It remains the task of the project manager (or perhaps the risk manager if one exists, acting on behalf of the project manager) to ensure that each risk is monitored and managed effectively.

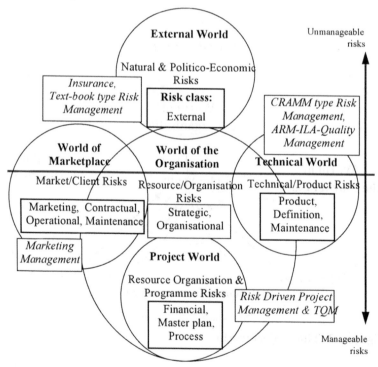

Figure 2.4 Types of risk and approaches developed for tackling them

In Figure 2.4 we show five 'homes' for risk. This is where they come from, where their causes lie, and with this understanding, one can quickly identify the individuals in the company who should take 'ownership' of them. This analysis formed the basis of the thinking of the *RISKMAN* team, which led to the process of classification and the twelve class table described in Section 2.1.7. However, before moving to that discussion, we will examine more fully three categories of risk in the section that follows.

2.1.6 Categories of project risk

In Section 2.1.1 we provided one clear definition of risk which was based on chance happenings of things going wrong. There can be a different case where nothing goes wrong as such, but there is uncertainty regarding how long something will take or how much it will cost. Take the simple example of the design of the cover of this book. Let us say that the designer estimates two days to settle the conceptual design. It is entirely conceivable that inspiration should come immediately and the design concept be settled in two hours. It is equally conceivable that he might be struggling to get some inspiration seven days later. This does not mean that the estimate is wrong in itself, or that he has suddenly become a bad designer. Many people would argue that this is not a matter of risk, simply of accuracy in estimating. Equally most would accept the explanation that there is in this case a significant **risk** of overrun against the design estimate! However, it is worth noting how this sort of risk is calculated. Here we calculate the allocation of reserve to cover the additional cost as a straight percentage of the original estimate. Again the issue is made more complex by the fact that a single value is not suitable to account for such a risk, and that instead we need a distribution curve. However, the most important point is that this represents a quite different category of risk with different characteristics. We will call this a *category one risk*.

Our initial definition in Section 2.1.1 provided a different calculation for a different sort of risk which was based on the cost of the contingency plan, rather than the estimate for the originally planned work. However, that sort of risk too is more complex than at first appears. That original definition was designed for when things go more significantly wrong, and there are at least two ways that this can happen which we will call *category two* and *category three risks*. In the first of these, things can go wrong which affect our estimates but not the main plan itself. In both cases we will be forced to take contingency action. The difference between the three categories is best illustrated by another example:

> Imagine that we have planned to fly from London to Lagos today in the company's aircraft. We estimated that it should take six hours and have

informed the office in Nigeria, arranging to be collected from the airport. Three things happen that fall one into each risk category:

1.   The weather is bad today. There will be storms and high winds (higher than the norm assumed in our estimate). The wind will be against us (which was expected), but we are likely to be as much as two hours late. We do not have to deviate from plan, indeed the problem is common enough to cause no surprise. There is little point in trying to inform Lagos since the typical telecommunications difficulties to Nigeria might delay our take-off and exacerbate the problem. The simplest thing is to get going and let the Lagos driver wait. The impact cost is 33% of the original time estimate plus any financial implications.

These financial implications may be considerable since we are rushing to an urgent meeting involving several highly paid members of the Company, but not to worry, it is usually like that with risk, and it cannot be helped.

We are facing a *category one risk*. No change to the original plan, but there is an impact cost. Our actual cost will vary significantly from estimate.

2.   Four hours into the flight and just as we cross the Atlas Mountains we hit a major storm (another *category one*) and the pilot has to climb above it. He contacts Marrakech Airport, which is quite close, to report his position and check on the weather ahead only to find that it is exceptionally bad, so much so that we would be wise to land, refuel and wait out the storms (this is the *category two*). We ask Marrakech to inform our office in Lagos that we are delayed, and continue climbing.

The impact cost includes the time of diversion and delay, plus extra fuel, (plus consequential additional costs of interfering with other people attending our meeting and which are now even greater).

Note this is not a calculation based on adding a percentage to the original estimate, but is the cost of the contingency action which is a new cost dependent on how far we happen to be from a suitable stopping place.

We have a *category two risk*. We are still basically on course, but things have gone wrong and we have to implement a contingency plan within the original plan. Our actual cost must include the even bigger variation from estimate plus the cost of the contingency activity.

3.   Half way through the climb one of the engines bursts into flame. Disconcerting but not really that bad. The automatic extinguishers douse the fire, the aircraft is designed to fly on the remaining engine, and we only have to get to Marrakech where they can fix the aircraft. However the repair might take days. In fact it is likely that we will transfer to scheduled flights, and leave the pilot to sort out the Company's aircraft.

We now have a *category three risk* and it is time to **change the original plan**. Throw away all past estimates to cover the last part of the flight and re-cost a new project plan.

The implications of these three categories are significant for the statistical approach to risk analysis. Categories one and two can both be modelled in deterministic (i.e. non-branching) networks, though the cost of the risk is calculated differently. However category three can only be modelled in a branching network or decision-tree.

The effects of the three categories on master plan, contingency plans, and costs are summarised in Figure 2.5.

Risk category	Risk effects		
	Master plan	Contingency	Cost
1	No	No	Yes
2	No	Yes	Yes
3	Yes	Yes	Yes

Figure 2.5 Risk impact by category

2.1.7 Classifying risk

In the same way that naturalists have developed a taxonomy of species in order to predict the characteristics and behaviour of living things, it is desirable to classify risks. This is useful because it provides pointers to who should be responsible for any given risk, where the risk's causes are likely to originate and this in turn leads to means by which that risk can be controlled.

Such classes must be tailored to each organisation (see Chapter 7). However, several rules must be followed:

- the classes must reflect the different specialisations involved on a project (finance, legal, technical, etc.);
- they must be representative of the various activities required to achieve the programme from the initial decision-making, through to operating the product;
- they must be compatible with the levels of decision-making inside the organisation;
- they should fit the four stages of configuration management (strategic, definition, technical and operation).

Milestone	Configur-ation	Risk class	Risk characterisation
Contract signature Product specification Product delivery	Strategic baseline	1. **Strategic**	Quality of the strategic plan. Likelihood of failure to achieve the strategic plan.
		2. **Marketing**	Quality of the requirements definition. Likelihood of failure to achieve the marketing plan. Commercial relations.
	Definition baseline	3. **Contractual**	Legal risks.
		4. **Financial**	Financial risks.
		5. **Master plan**	Likelihood of failure to meet major milestones and costs.
		6. **Definition**	Likelihood of failure to meet the product requirements.
	Technical baseline	7. **Process (WBS)**	Implementing a particular process.
		8. **Product (PBS)**	Developing a particular architecture.
		9. **Organisation (OBS)**	Managing the organisation.
	Operation baseline	10. **Operational**	Harm or injury caused by product operation.
		11. **Maintenance**	Cost of maintenance.
		12. **External**	Problems created by, or for, the environment or socio-political world.

Figure 2.6 Classification of risk

This last rule is of the utmost importance. It enables the classes to be associated with the project life-cycle process through which a user requirement is identified, and progressively transformed into a project concept, a tangible project, and finally a product. Traditionally, four *baselines* are established during this process:

the strategic baseline: encapsulates the perception and requirements of the outside world, especially user, customer and funder, taking cognisance of the market and the competition. The potential routes to achieve identified targets such as market positioning, profit, and product portfolio, must be reviewed and the means required to follow these routes, including overall financing resources, etc. A particular project may be analysed at this level, either to examine its fit within the strategic plan (opportunity) or to define it as part of the means to achieve the plan (internal investment and/or development).

the definition baseline: concerns the particular route settled upon to achieve the project requirements. It is the target in terms of high-level product design, function and performance, the costs involved, the contractual aspects and the plan committed.

the technical baseline: is the response to the definition baseline requirements, which embodies finalising the design of the product architecture and its implementation, and the means of ensuring that it satisfies the definition requirements.

the operation baseline: is developed to cover the period after the product is delivered and provides mechanisms for its maintenance, operation and enhancement.

Of course, each of these major stages involve risks, and in Figure 2.6 we give examples of risk classes associated with them, and expand with a brief description of the characteristics that will give rise to the risk.

Classification applies to both risk impacts, and risk causes; however, they differ in their relationship in one important respect. It should be possible to position each risk impact in only one class in the table On the other hand, one risk may have many causes which exist in other classes. When a risk impact or cause can be ascribed to more than one class, it should be possible, and is desirable, to break that impact or cause down into two or more constituents, each of which can be allocated to one and only one class. This will ease the task of ascribing ownership of the risk. The risk owner will only be able to control his risk through action taken by the various individuals responsible for the risk's causes (see Figure 2.2).

When the *RISKMAN* methodology is implemented in any given environment, one of the first tasks is to develop a list of the primary risk areas likely to be of concern in that environment. This is then reviewed against the classification table to help amplify and elaborate the list, which then leads to the development of cause-effect diagrams (see Figure 3.10). These have been found to be particularly beneficial early in the project life-cycle when risk information is both sparse, and difficult to generate.

A tailored list based on this classification proves very useful in developing checklists and guidance for staff charged with identifying and quantifying risk. The classification mechanism has been found to be both powerful and effective. As each risk is identified, participants in the process are forced to be methodical and specific. As the risk is classified, these participants inevitably reflect on contingency plans and mitigation strategies, and are automatically led on to allocating responsibility and so on.

2.2 Difficulties with risk management

RISKMAN provides a structured approach to overcoming the difficulties of risk management.   In order to use it successfully, it is necessary to clearly understand what those difficulties are, and how they combine exponentially to create the overall problem of project risk which is so difficult to manage that it has made the development and documentation of *RISKMAN* necessary.

We have already discussed three difficulties with risk.   In Section 1.4 we discussed the first problem:

- Engineering and development staff are often (and justifiably) distrustful of senior management concerning risk so that they are unwilling to communicate with honesty their extensive experience of the risks that the company is taking.   This problem means that not only do staff need training in techniques for analysing and communicating risk information, but senior managements need to be convinced of their own need for education in correctly interpreting that data, and building confidence in their subordinates to provide it.

In Section 2.1.2 we explained that:

- Identifying and quantifying risk is about trying to forecast the unknown, and in a sense the unknowable. That one can only know for certain that a risk event will occur in hindsight, i.e. after it has occurred and ceased to be a risk. That only then will one be certain of the cumulative effect of risk occurrences thus far in any project, and that information is never complete until the project is finished and the information is of no further value from a management point of view.

In Section 2.1.6 we described a third difficulty:

- At a detailed level there are three categories of risk which need to be handled differently. The first one is calculated differently from the rest, and the other two can only be simulated in different types of models.

We need in this section to draw the reader's attention to three further problems or groups of problems:

- First we will draw attention to difficulties which arise because risk provisioning is inextricably bound up with the main plan for the project.

- Secondly we will discuss the common misconceptions about the extent with which risk can be passed on or shared with suppliers, sub-contractors, customers, partners, or insurers.

- Thirdly we wish to examine critically the current tendency to turn to the computer for a solution. New offerings of software to analyse risk have become fashionable, and many consultants, academics and statisticians are moving into this field. The problem of accumulating many interacting variables in a statistical way is complex, and the only practical means to do so is to turn to the computerised solution. However, this process has many more practical difficulties than theoretical ones. In the *RISKMAN* scheme of things it is recommended very rarely, and should be used with caution. This position adopted by the *RISKMAN* team has caused surprise in some quarters, but has been taken after much discussion amongst the team which was composed of both statistical experts and experienced project professionals.

Finally in this section we will look at practical means of managing risk which takes these problems into account. Whilst the statistical validity of these approaches may be criticised by the statistics expert or operational researcher, they have been found to be both practical and useful, and are much favoured by project professionals who have to face the practical problems of risk management.

2.2.1 The project plan contains what you are not going to do

Everyone assumes, when developing a plan, that they are deciding what they are going to do. In a project situation this assumption is totally invalid. Consider the project of sailing from Dublin to New York.

> An experienced sailor sets out with a chart on which a line indicating the planned route is marked (Figure 2.7 (a)). Navigational equipment is used to plot the course throughout the trip. This is because the sailor does **not** expect to travel precisely along the planned route. Throughout the trip readings are taken to establish position, anticipating that adjustments to direction will be needed. The plan is actually **more** important than if the sailor were going to adhere precisely to that plan.

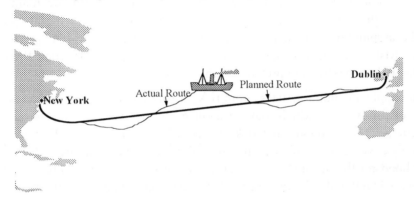

Figure 2.7 (a) The baseline plan

The sailor needs to refer to the chart each time that the course is changed. The chart is both the yardstick used to decide whether to change course, and the means by which the new course is chosen. It is worth noting the direction change shown in Figure 2.8. This does not head directly for the target. Neither does it take the shortest route to get back on plan. It takes a direction which is likely to lead directly to the target assuming that prevailing conditions of wind, tide and current which have affected the journey recently will not change immediately. Note also that the original line on the chart is left for reference.

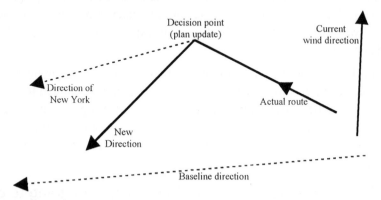

Figure 2.8 Adjustments to plan (changing course)

In project management terms the original planned route is the *budget baseline* against which the efficiency of his sailing decisions will be judged unless a new baseline is set. The current course is the latest project plan, and is constantly changing. The baseline only changes if there is a major review where such a change is agreed, or if the project terms of reference themselves are changed. A major review can be forced by significant risk happenings such as storm damage forcing our sailor to put in to Newfoundland for repairs. This would involve incorporating a contingency plan which makes a significant impact on overall time, cost and/or quality, into the main plan. However, the important thing from a risk standpoint is that each plan is made on the assumption that there is uncertainty with regard to what will happen next. Risk is not just a matter of contingency planning for when things go wrong, risk is inextricably bound into the main plan itself.

Most people, including writers about risk, presume that the risk budget is there to cater for all costs which may be incurred but whose necessity is currently uncertain. That is to say that risk events are not entered into the main plan, but only covered in stand-by plans. In reality this is far from the truth. A high likelihood for the occurrence of such a risk event is assumed to be, say, 90%. In fact, when the likelihood exceeds 50%, the occurrence is clearly more likely than not. In these circumstances, virtually every project manager will want to see such an occurrence catered for in the main plan rather than the risk budget! Taking the converse of this statement, there are likely to be some items in the main plan with up to 50% likelihood of not being needed. Whether the break-point for such items should be 50%, 70%, or 40% is very much a matter for individual preference. Previous comments on the impossibility of accuracy in forecasting probability of occurrence makes setting a fixed number for this a relatively academic point anyway. However, whilst *RISKMAN* does not take a specific position on any particular number, it does require the issue to be confronted.

The implications of this situation are that, buried in any project plan, there are likely to be positive risk occurrences which will yield funds to the risk budget if it transpires that they are not required. Exhaustive risk forecasting would involve identifying these items and raising negative values in the risk budget to cater for them. This level of thoroughness may be desirable in those few cases where the item concerned is costly. However, it is rarely done in practice, and is not recommended as a matter of course in the *RISKMAN* methodology. Nevertheless, acknowledging this state of affairs and yet not attempting to measure its significance can make nonsense of attempts to measure risk accurately and therefore it is specified as a requirement in the most comprehensive applications of *RISKMAN*. The main lesson from this statement is confirmation that risk analysis is not an accurate science, and that the cost of doing the risk analysis itself should be weighed against the likely significance of its outcome.

2.2.2 Difficulties in sharing or delegating risk

A most common strategy for risk avoidance is to pass the risk to an organisation better able to manage it. This is a tactic much recommended within *RISKMAN*. A risk is clearly safest in the hands of those best qualified to manage it, those with maximum control over its causes. Having said this, it is important to appreciate that the process is the same as the delegation of responsibility in management terms, and is subject to the same limitations.

The process of delegation involves giving away the authority to act, and once delegated, this authority can not be taken back without undermining the person or body to whom authority was delegated. However, whilst authority must be given away, the corresponding responsibility cannot be totally passed on in the same way. Having delegated, the delegator remains responsible for the result, even though the recipient of the authority in future also shares responsibility for the outcome. A similar situation arises when risk is passed on, and whilst the risk is reduced by the process, any adverse effects of the risk occurring can rarely be avoided totally.

Once a contract is established, it is in the interest of both parties that the contract should be met. When a customer writes penalty clauses into a contract for late delivery, he does not do so because he wants to save money, he does so because he wants delivery on time. (When the supplier is late he will suffer loss of income.) Whilst this will benefit the customer by reducing the price, the reduction is not likely to compensate for the inconvenience or opportunity cost that the customer is incurring. We have here a lose-lose situation. Equally, when delivery is made on time, the customer pays more and the supplier, hopefully, makes a handsome profit. At the same time, the customer benefits from having full use of the product on time and we have a win-win situation. Both customer and supplier share the results of the cost/benefit equation with risk occurrences.

Imagine the situation where a supplier is delivering a delicate prototype for testing, and it is at risk of damage in transit. As a result, insurance is taken out to cover the item. There is indeed damage in transit and a claim is made on the insurer. Nobody wins in this case. Whilst the actual costs of the prototype may be recovered, this is most unlikely to cover the damage done by disruption of schedules, etc.

It is a mistake on the part of customers to believe that they can avoid risk by making their suppliers cover the cost. In a commercial world, the supplier has to make the customer pay in the long run, or he will go out of business. When a supplier takes a risk, he should, and will, put up his price to cover that risk. The whole basis of risk management is that he should do just this, and then manage the risks so well that he converts the price supplement into additional profit. This is not corruption or racketeering, it is sound professional management, always has been, and is not going to change: if you take the risk, you should reap the benefit or bear the cost. Any customer who wants you to bear the cost if there is one, but pass on any benefit if there is one, is trying to both eat his cake and keep it.

2.2.3 Difficulties with the statistical approach

Many of the specialists in risk who offer consultancy and/or publish papers and books on the subject, are either academics or professional consultants who have associated themselves with a particular software product. Virtually all risk software products on the market use variations of the *Monte Carlo* method for summarising the cumulative effect of consequential variables. This is, indeed, the only way to accurately perform this task.

The results of the computer work performed by the risk specialists can be most impressive and quite exciting for senior management, as may be seen from Figure 2.9. However, we have some fundamental criticisms of their approach which can be itemised as follows:

- The data input to risk analysis tools is inevitably inaccurate, incomplete, and very much over-simplified.

- Exhaustive (and expensive) accurate processing of this poor-quality data using powerful computers is, to say the least, precarious.

- The more detailed and impressive the computer-produced results, the more management are seduced into believing them. This makes decision-making even more precarious.

- Whilst the risk specialists may fully understand the complexities of risk in projects, they often do not do very well when it comes to explaining what they know.

Cost/Schedule Out-turn Envelopes

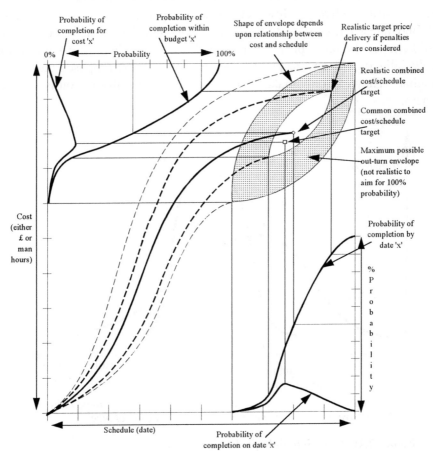

Figure 2.9 Cost/Schedule out-turn envelopes

In summary, there are usually good reasons why a sophisticated analysis is unsuitable, particularly as it can be expensive and time-consuming. This is recognised within the *RISKMAN* methodology in the provision of three levels of application: Basic, Intermediate and Comprehensive *RISKMAN*, which will be further described in Chapter 3. In the latter application level, the use of sophisticated models to obtain improved presentation of the range of risk exposure assists senior management in reaching key strategic decisions on exposure levels acceptable to the company.

We have been very critical of an exhaustive application of the statistical approach to risk analysis which is currently in vogue. It should be said that there are situations where this approach is justified and worthwhile. Take for example a development project with two design options, for which the cost and /or schedule probability curves have profiles shaped as shown in Figure 2.10. Clearly the lower profile (alternative 1) offers the possibility of a lower cost and earlier delivery. However it is also capable of providing the highest cost and latest delivery. Most managements faced with data such as this would choose the taller profile, which will give them the best assurance of a timely delivery with an acceptable cost, even though the proposed target price is higher. They can only make such a decision if the information is available to them.

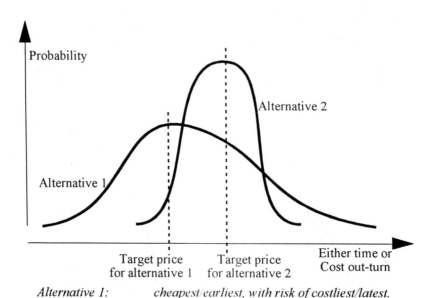

| Alternative 1: | cheapest/earliest, with risk of costliest/latest. |
| Alternative 2: | lower risk and more reliable choice. |

Figure 2.10 Cost/Schedule probability curves

Sadly, it is unlikely that information which could provide the picture shown, could ever be acquired. Whilst the risk analysts are seeking to deliver useful information to management with the best of intentions, it is our opinion that all too often they are indulging in *GIGO - garbage in, garbage out*. A major reason for this is that engineers will persist in hiding risk contingency as we have described earlier. Meanwhile, the information which is fed into our risk analysis tools may be significantly more inaccurate than the base estimates which themselves usually cause major problems. Whilst an engineer can guess with reasonable accuracy how long a job will take, he has great difficulty in predicting the probability curve for its completion. Similarly, he can provide contingency plans for risk occurrences and cost them quite reasonably, but when it comes to assessing the probability of their occurrence, he is most unlikely to provide realistic data.

The true complexity of modelling a major project can be illustrated by the following sequence (the diagrams in Figures 2.11 and 2.12 use the activity-on-arrow schematic):

- Take a typical deterministic CPM network and lay it flat (note that it is only deterministic in the sense that it provides only one option for planned activities).

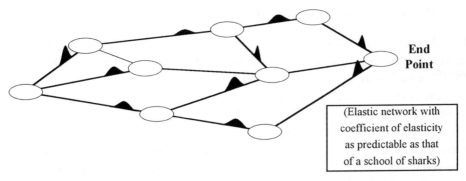

End Point

(Elastic network with coefficient of elasticity as predictable as that of a school of sharks)

Figure 2.11 Modelling category 1 and 2 risks

- All estimates of time and cost on the original network have uncertainty in their value and each estimate will vary with a probability distribution, as shown (picture the activities as oscillating lengths of elastic). This means lots of potential critical paths.

- Superimpose risk decision trees on the vertical plane within this network.

- Each of the risk decision points requires an alternative network to be drawn out (each network is as elastic as any other CPM network).

- Some of these networks interact.

- Consequential risks confuse the issue further.

- External events and constraints impact the model, and they have to be modelled too.

- All these combinations of things culminate in the one agreed end point determined by the project terms of reference.

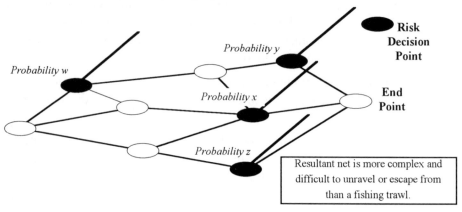

Probability w

Probability y

Probability x

Probability z

Risk Decision Point

End Point

Resultant net is more complex and difficult to unravel or escape from than a fishing trawl.

Figure 2.12 Modelling category 3 risk

It is clear from this analysis that bottom-up estimating and modelling of risk is more difficult and expensive than the most comprehensive implementation of PERT, which only fell out of favour because it was so demanding of project support resource. This leads to the conclusion that a top-down approach to project risk modelling is preferable. Parametric estimating[8] is rarely thought of as a tool for risk modelling, but in practice it is potentially far more efficient and useful - especially when extended to include whole-life costing and reliability - than Monte Carlo[9] simulations based on bottom-up detailed data. It is likely that this situation will change as maturity levels in risk management increase, and low-cost computing provides knowledge-based and artificial intelligence systems to facilitate continuous improvement in project environments. However, at the present time, the statistical approach supported by available computerised tools should be used with a top-down philosophy, taking care to treat the resulting outputs with due caution.

2.2.4 Taking account of the problems

Having looked at some of the problems encountered in quantifying risk, it may seem that we can only recommend a qualitative approach. This must not

[8]Parametric estimating will be discussed fully in the *RISKMAN* manuals.

[9]Monte Carlo simulation is discussed briefly in the appendix on risk modelling.

be the case. If we are going to manage risk pro-actively, it is essential that we quantify it. Only by that means can we make rational decisions about how much time and money to spend in doing so. The problems are severe, but they have to be overcome. So the question now is, "How can we quantify risk despite these problems?"

The only realistic answer is to keep a balanced view, and ensure that one is not trying to achieve an accuracy level which is impossible. One should stick to the simpler techniques whenever one can, moving to the more exhaustive techniques only when the riskiness of the project indicates that it is necessary. When one is forced to measure overall risk more thoroughly, do so at a fairly high level. Variants of the Monte Carlo method can work very well when applied in a top-down manner at a fairly high level.

The danger of the Garbage In, Garbage Out syndrome builds rapidly when the approach is applied at low levels. Once one loses sight of the overall picture because of the weight of the detail, then things can get out of control.

So if approximate numbers, rapidly processed in a small model, can provide useful information, what is the size of model one should aim for? It seems that a network model of thirty or forty activities is a good target. There are people who argue that with such a small model, one does not need a sophisticated method for processing the data. Again, the specific details of each individual situation are likely to make either one or other of these positions valid.

One has to maintain this balanced view throughout the different phases of the project, building more detail into a solid base. Using the work breakdown structure approach, one must recognise that some degree of risk is catered for in the main plan, but that additional risk reserve is likely to be needed. Whilst a very long list of risks may be desirable for risk monitoring and control, if they are all quantified and contribute to the risk reserve, the total cost picture is likely to be unacceptable and unreasonably high. It is therefore likely that the actual risk reserve will be calculated from a fairly small selection of the major risks. The statistical justification for this approach is small or non-existent, but it works.

At the end of the day, the project manager must feel comfortable with the total budget allocation and be confident that he can deliver the goods with that resource level. So we must conclude that professional risk management is a strange mixture of exhaustive and detailed analysis to ensure that one is keeping an eye on all the risks, tempered with a large amount of individual judgement based on experience.

2.3 Developments in project management thinking

This section is a worthy subject for a volume should any research students be interested. It will, of necessity, be full of generalisations and should not be taken too literally. For example, when discussing the topic of *Quality Management* and placing it firmly in the time period of the 1980s, the authors are aware that the history of the *Total Quality Management* movement can be traced back to the 1940s and beyond. However, the great impact that quality management advocates achieved in the boardroom was first felt strongly in the 1980s. Similar statements could be made about ARM (Availability, Reliability and Maintainability), etc. The story of the development of project management thinking is large and complex and difficult to simplify, so we will try to tell this story in chronological order, simply to give it some order, and we will structure it in decades from 1950. Therefore the section will be structured as follows:

pre-1950: the era of unstructured common sense

the 1950s: the decade of Scientific Management

the 1960s: the decade of Project Planning Techniques

the 1970s: the decade of Project Control Techniques

the 1980s: the decade of Excellence?

the 1990s and beyond: *Management by Project*

As Steve Marsh has said in the Preface to this book, we are living through a time of great change. Many thinkers have likened it to the great epochs which are milestones in the evolution of man, such as the *Agricultural Revolution*, the *Urban Revolution* and the *Industrial Revolution*, and now people talk of the *Information Revolution* or the *Information Technology Revolution*, which has been taking place since the 1950s and has not yet ended. It is no accident that project management thinking should evolve through a quantum leap in conjunction with this period of great change. Applying Darwin's theory to the evolution of our species and our society, this is exactly what has been required in order for progress to take place.

The zenith of the *Industrial Revolution* was embodied in Henry Ford's production line. This allowed human activities to be isolated and repeated endlessly to build skill to a pitch which maximised the efficiency of workers' efforts. This in turn meant that the automation which was the foundation of industrialisation could be applied in a new way which completely dispensed with the need for a worker at all, and we arrived at the *Information Revolution*. However, that was just a starting point, and automation is now being applied to clerical tasks and even management tasks where they are repetitive. This development has created the question of the century, which is, *What are people going to do for a living in future?*

The answer is that people will be doing only those things which cannot be done more efficiently by computers and robots. This in turn means that the input to the management process required by business will be creative activities which must be done on a *one-off* basis. We refer you again to the *Spectrum of Production and Operations Environments* and point out that this means **projects**. Management in the immediate future is going to increasingly focus on projects as the fundamental units of management activity, and good business managers will be those that understand what projects are all about. Thus the future will be in *management by project*.

It is hardly surprising that there has been an explosion of theories and texts about project management, this volume being yet another. Human tasks in the next phase of business evolution will be creative tasks, and management tasks. Management tasks will consist of:

(i)   Communication with management support information systems to make non-repetitive decisions that the system cannot make itself.

(ii)   Performing project management tasks which are currently outside the scope of even the most modern project management support systems.

Amazingly the systems which are of least practical help to managers at present are those which purport to support the project manager. Since there are more than a hundred software packages currently on the market claiming to be *project management systems*, this needs some explanation.

2.3.1 Pre-1950: the era of unstructured common sense

Historically, project management was not seen as a career path, rather it was what engineers did in order to build the things that they designed. Not long ago if you filled a room with 50 project managers and asked them what is their profession?, you would get a wide selection of answers like: I am a Civil Engineer, or a Naval Architect, or an Aerodynamicist, or a Systems Developer. Hardly one would be likely to describe himself with his real job title. Even today, projects are still commonly confused with their product and not seen as the process through which the product is delivered.

Throughout this long period of history, projects were achieved by the application of common sense, and little thought was given to the process, or to making sure that it was performed efficiently. Indeed, the typical project manager of today entered the profession because he wanted to build bridges or ships or aircraft or systems. This has always been a major problem. Project managers have usually received many years of training and skills development in their chosen profession, but are promoted to project manager with relatively little attention given to their skill in budgeting, negotiating, man management or even scheduling. Many project managers count themselves lucky if they have had as much as a week's training in the disciplines required by their job.

There was one shining light in this period from a man called Gantt who invented a scheduling method around the turn of the century. His technique is widely used and known as *bar charting*. It is in fact very powerful as a scheduling tool enabling the experienced professional to visualise when things will occur, and manually adjust the schedule to ensure that it makes sense. Unfortunately, it is largely thought of as a communications mechanism, and seen as the output of a project scheduling system which is invariably less efficient than the brains of the professionals who use its data.

2.3.2 The 1950s: the decade of Scientific Management

The onset of the *Cold War*, coming immediately after World War II when the super powers had got into the habit of accepting massive military expenditure, created an environment in which huge project budgets were allocated to the arms race and then the space race. Being a race, time was of the essence. The cultural and organisational problems we have described in Section 1.4, plus the increased complexity of the products themselves, led procurement executives to become dissatisfied with continual failure to meet optimistic delivery targets.

Consultants and theorists were challenged to improve the situation, the operational researchers had a field day, and P.E.R.T. (*Programme Evaluation and Review Technique*) was born. In its original form, it was actually an attempt to grapple with the real problem of project scheduling - which is uncertainty. It required estimates of the earliest possible, the most likely, and the most pessimistic duration of activities in a project. They were fed into a network diagram which established the logic of the order in which those activities had to take place. A statistically-derived formula was used to modify the most likely target and make it more pessimistic.

In hindsight, it is fair to say that the development of PERT tended to create one real problem and accidentally created a far larger one.

The first problem was that advocates tried to use the network to model the project in great detail. This is necessary to make the technique truly accurate. However, it also creates a need for a large amount of clerical effort, and results in such a complex network that it is difficult to manage. Indeed, had it not been for the advent of computers and the *Information Revolution*, then it is most likely that Critical Path Analysis, the surviving relative of PERT, would have died in the decade that it was born. Indeed, PERT itself has rarely been used in its true form, and the contributions that it made to the project management profession were that it helped in the acceptance of networking and that it gave its name to the first computer system to utilise networking. The actual name PERT has since been applied very loosely until it can no longer be assumed to mean a genuine attempt to grapple with uncertainty.

The accidental problem has resulted from the need for a computer system to support the use of networking. From the late 1960s onwards, a myriad of software offerings based on networking have poured onto the market calling themselves *project management systems*. In reality, they are nothing of the kind, but are mostly aids to activity scheduling which is but a small part of the whole job of managing a project. The systems development world has become so involved with this particular technique that they have tried to bend their systems endlessly to cover the needs of the project manager in order to maintain the networking technique as the foundation. Whilst this turn of events can hardly be blamed on the developers of PERT, it has been a very unfortunate one.

2.3.3 The 1960s: the decade of Project Planning Techniques

The 1960s saw attempts to apply critical path analysis in many other areas than just defence, particularly in the oil industry. It was quickly found that whilst the initial problem for the project scheduler was to order the activities he scheduled, the main problem was the constraint of the availability of relevant resources to perform the activity at the time it was scheduled. Systems developers rapidly turned their attention to devising resource scheduling rules with which to restrict the use of the pure logic of the network. Large amounts of development effort were wasted on this search for the *Holy Grail* of the perfect scheduler. In real life, resource scheduling is only effective when it includes such transient rules as:

> Tony is better at that job than Ned;
>
> Sarah needs a change from that kind of work;
>
> Bill's wife is having a baby and his productivity is likely to drop during the next eight months.

After all those years of systems effort, most automatically generated project schedules can still be improved by many a shopfloor worker using a Gantt chart with experience and knowledge of the company.

Whilst the systems people were failing to achieve automatic resource scheduling, it became clear that management's primary interest was still what it always has been, namely cost. Project management systems were instantly modified further. Facilities were added to allow resources and activities to be costed, but these facilities were hardly used since the whole project industry fell into one of two categories:

(i)   those who used the quantity surveyor approach to costing, and

(ii)   those belonging to the group that were already moving towards formal *Work Breakdown Structures*.

The 1960s also saw the first moves towards an emphasis on control rather than planning, with the primary drive for that control being cost issues, the secondary drive being schedule issues and the acknowledgement that schedule control can only be achieved through resource control. This set the scene for the *Cost Time and Resource* (CTR) systems which would be developed by the oil industry in the late 1970s and early 1980s. However, the heart of this movement was the rise of *Work Breakdown Structures* as a proposed basis for project management systems, supported by *Earned Value Performance Monitoring* as the control mechanism. The basic thinking on *Work Breakdown Structures* originated from the British Ministry of Defence at the end of the 1960s[10].

2.3.4 The 1970s: the decade of Project Control Techniques

The 1970s saw parallel developments in the defence arena and oil industry. The first to move, however, were the defence procurement agencies, who by this time were grappling with the problems of *Cost-Plus Development Contracts*, and the need to get value for taxpayers' money. This resulted in the publication of *Cost/Schedule Control Systems Criteria* (C/SCSC) by the Department of Defense in the USA. This turn of events was motivated by the most forward looking and constructive thinking in the period covered in the decades of our story. However, it was to be frustrated in its results by defence manufacturers who had a vested interest in staying on cost plus contracts where their profitability was guaranteed. Computer support systems developers failed to grasp the significance, and instead of developing modern systems from scratch with the WBS as the foundation, and networking as nothing more that a supporting technique, they tried yet again to bend their already deformed project management systems to accommodate yet another fresh set of requirements. Meanwhile, defence manufacturers paid lip-service to compliance with C/SCSC requirements.

The oil industry was by this time the big spender on project management systems development. Systems suppliers seized the opportunity created by the advent of the mini-computer to land large lucrative contracts to re-invent the wheel, and came up with CTR systems which had a very similar

---

[10]Report from the Steering Group on Development Cost Estimating, Volume 2: Handbook of Procedures: Programming, Estimating and Control of Development Processes.

philosophical base to C/SCSC systems. The main difference between the two being that CTR systems focused attention on control of sub-contracts and assumed a legal framework which involved a *prime contractor*, or *managing contractor* controlling a myriad of *sub-contractors*. In this sense CTR systems could be said to be more modern and to anticipate the needs of future decades, but in all other senses they merely arrived later at the end of the decade.

By this time, inventing clever new techniques with impressive names had become accepted as the way to be modern and make progress. Meanwhile, *project management systems* had become accepted as being network-based planning systems, which became confused with the expression *project management* itself. A whole series of techniques sprang up to satisfy the additional needs of real project managers, but they had to be given names which did not use the phrase *project management*. Suddenly there were *Configuration Management* techniques and systems; *Parametric Estimating* techniques and systems; *Availability Reliability Maintainability and Safety* techniques and systems (ARM and Safety), and more. The specialists in these areas needed to establish their own career paths, and did not want to answer to the Project Planning Manager, whose department was often misnamed the *Project Management Office,* so they would deny avidly that they were anything to do with the old fashioned business of *project management.*

2.3.5 The 1980s: the decade of Excellence?

The 1980s were dominated by attempts amongst consultants, theorists and researchers to discover the magic ingredient of Japanese economic success, and make money by selling it around the Western World. They sold all sorts of new techniques, most of which had only the most tenuous link with the reason for Japanese success, including *Quality Circles* (small groups of people who were encouraged to talk to each other), and *Just-in-Time* (which originally meant having only one supplier for major components, and many deliveries per day of specified quantities). The latter clearly related to mass manufacturing, and was irrelevant to the project environment, though its name misled many project buyers into believing they were using the most modern of techniques. Few of these techniques had any significant impact on management thinking, until a book was published entitled *In Search of Excellence*[11]. This book directed attention at the need to focus on the customer, and provide real customer satisfaction. The *excellence movement* coincided with a fashion for quality management and registration under

---

[11]*In Search of Excellence* by Thomas J. Peters and Robert H. Waterman Jr., published by Harper and Row, New York, in 1982.

BS5750/ISO9000[12]. This development clearly brought many benefits, though it also carries with it some dangers which are still largely unrecognised. An aspect of this movement has been a new insistence on documented procedures, and this has significant implications for the world of project management.

Project-based companies suffer from the effects of the business cycle in a strange way. Either they have lots of contracts with delivery deadlines and no time to develop procedures, or they have insufficient contracts and everyone is so busy bidding that they have no time to invest in speculative activity such as procedure writing. The 1980s saw a move to counter this syndrome as a result of a movement towards *Programmes Management* which started in the American defence arena. With a *Programmes Management* approach, individual projects are grouped together under a programme manager who is a sort of super project manager, managing families of products from cradle to grave, and the *Programmes Office* offers a secure career path for the project manager. The movement has led to the development and documentation of a structured approach to project management. Nowadays many managements have, or are developing, project procedures which comply with the quality standards, and fit in to the new strategic direction their company is taking.

The 1980s also saw significant attempts to improve the design process. Whilst the 1970s had led to expressions like *design to cost* and *ARM and safety*, the 1980s saw variations such as *Design to Whole-Life Cost* and *Integrated Logistics Analysis* (ILA) and *Support* (ILS). With whole-life costing, attention is paid to minimise the downstream costs of use, maintenance and disposal of the product, even if this means a relatively small increase in the development cost, so that maximum value is achieved for the customer. With ILA/ILS, individuals with experience of maintenance and support are recruited into the development team and trained to use their experience to improve the design and optimise the whole-life cost.

Attempts to improve the design process, particularly in the area of systems development, led to a reassessment of the project life cycle. If the phases of the project life-cycle are viewed as a continuous cascade then a significant feedback loop is missed. However, if the design process is seen as a cascade of phases like a flight of steps going down, and the development process is seen as a corresponding flight of steps going up, then the cross links from step to step show where the feedback process is most relevant. This was described as the *V-Diagram* by Putman *et al.* When this thinking is laid alongside the ILA/ILS approach, a consistent theme becomes clear, and an important aspect of this theme is a return to a focus of attention on the product.

---

[12]BS5750 and ISO9000 are the two identical sets of quality management standards issued by the British Standards Institute, and the International Standards Organisation.

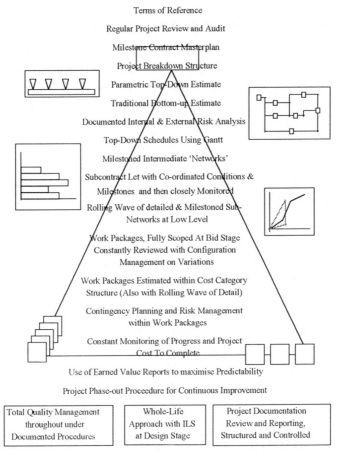

Terms of Reference

Regular Project Review and Audit

Milestone Contract Masterplan

Project Breakdown Structure

Parametric Top-Down Estimate

Traditional Bottom-up Estimate

Documented Internal & External Risk Analysis

Top-Down Schedules Using Gantt

Milestoned Intermediate 'Networks'

Subcontract Let with Co-ordinated Conditions &
Milestones and then closely Monitored

Rolling Wave of detailed & Milestoned Sub-
Networks at Low Level

Work Packages, Fully Scoped At Bid Stage
Constantly Reviewed with Configuration
Management on Variations

Work Packages Estimated within Cost Category
Structure (Also with Rolling Wave of Detail)

Contingency Planning and Risk Management
within Work Packages

Constant Monitoring of Progress and Project
Cost To Complete

Use of Earned Value Reports to maximise Predictability

Project Phase-out Proceedure for Continuous Improvement

Total Quality Management throughout under Documented Procedures	Whole-Life Approach with ILS at Design Stage	Project Documentation Review and Reporting, Structured and Controlled

Figure 2.13 State of the art project management techniques

The importance of the product, as well as the process to be managed by the project manager is also evident in the methodologies for project management which first became fashionable in the 1980s, and this is a major contribution of the *PRINCE Methodology* sponsored by the CCTA in the UK[13]. A further major contribution of PRINCE was the re-emphasis of the need to clearly identify and document the requirements of the project, and to apply strict configuration management, not just to the product, but to the project itself.

The 1980s also saw a fashion for yet more techniques. Those most relevant to this volume are the risk analysis techniques and the increased attention on risk engineering, which are more than adequately described in other parts of this book. Software tools also burgeoned in this period, though most were still based on nothing better than conventional network analysis.

---

[13] *The PRINCE Methodology*, NCC Blackwell Ltd., 1990.

2.3.6 The 1990s and beyond: *Management by Project*

We have now come up to the present day. Having started with project management being achieved in an *ad hoc* manner using common sense and experience, our story has shown the departure from a practical approach to a search for techniques, and a steady movement back to a practical approach, but this time based on sound theory and a clear structure.

The term *Management by Project* reflects the notion that all the key activities that govern the success or failure of a company or enterprise are now rightly identified as projects, and the effective management of the company consists largely of the effective management of those projects.

It was only when attention returned to uncertainty and risk that the proper place of planning became clear. The world of project management is now ready to stop using the project plan as a big stick to beat the project manager whenever their projects exhibit incidental variations from that plan. We are ready to take a pro-active and effective attitude to the identification and management of risk, but it is clear that one must first follow the rules and learn the lessons of the last forty years. There must be a plan to achieve the project objectives embodied in a structured project breakdown with allocated responsibility.   Techniques representing the current *state of the art* are summarised in Figure 2.13, and this must be seen as a basis for *RISKMAN*. Having that basis is a prerequisite for *RISKMAN*'s success.

2.4 Requirements for a better approach

We have attempted in this chapter to provide an understanding of the concept of risk, to examine some of the problems which it involves, to relate it to the project environment. In the last chapter we looked at the current position in an attempt to establish how much it needs changing. Whilst there are many positive trends, the situation can still benefit from further improvement. It is clear that there is a great deal that has to be done to ensure that risk is managed professionally even in the most well-established project-based companies.   We now wish to examine the requirements of that better approach, the requirements for *RISKMAN*. We will group these under six headings.

2.4.1 Compatibility with the project world

The approach needs to be constructed to integrate smoothly into the project environment. Risk management must, at no time, be seen as a separate activity from the management of the project overall, but rather should be embedded in the project management process.

2.4.2 Flexibility

Projects vary greatly from the large complex major development involving massive expenditure to the small and relatively mundane. The approach must be flexible, and enable the level of risk management sophistication to be matched to the project's needs.

Managements wanting to adopt the approach are likely to vary significantly in their risk management maturity. The approach must be sophisticated enough to be of immediate use to mature managements, but also flexible enough to provide simple and effective guidance for the newly initiated.

The approach should also be capable of leading staff at all levels through a development process as they gain experience of risk management.

2.4.3 Visibility

The first requirement for an effective risk management process to take place is that there is clear visibility of the information needed for sound decision-making. The approach must provide an efficient means to ensure that the right risks are identified, qualified, quantified, documented and analysed. Visibility must then be maintained during the life of a project, monitoring the status of all risks taken, and reporting all significant risk developments.

2.4.4 Ownership

If any approach is to achieve genuine control of risk, it is essential that ownership of each risk is clearly allocated to one appropriate person, and that separate ownership is also ascribed to each cause of that risk. The risk owner must have the power to act in control of the risk, and must report action taken through the relevant channels, which are to the project manager/risk manager concerning developments in his risk area. He also needs to know and liaise with all 'owners' of risk causes.

2.4.5 Understanding and strategy development

The methodology must make provision for identifying risk management skills and educating/training all relevant staff regarding risk. Those staff must develop a real understanding of risk causes, and the skill to construct and implement risk mitigation strategies.

2.4.6 Continuous improvement

Not only should the implementation of the approach establish a comprehensive knowledge base of the project risks regularly faced by the organisation, but also it should provide for the continual up-date and improvement of risk knowledge and skill. A mechanism for the capture of corporate information must be embodied, and the modification of procedures to accommodate the exploitation of that knowledge must also be built in to the approach. This may require the imposition of a risk maturity audit procedure similar to that required by ISO9000 for quality management. Indeed, for project-oriented companies, the auditing process may be combined.

3
The *RISKMAN* Approach

Risk management is an integral part of good project management. The *RISKMAN* project risk management process that is introduced in this chapter, effectively develops and expands the project management function. It describes the activities required to identify and control the causes and impacts of risks and the integration of these to form a risk-driven management process. A company that adopts the *RISKMAN* methodology and incorporates it into its management style and culture should reduce the likelihood of contracts turning into disasters, or, if things do go wrong it will ensure that a management process is in place to get early warning and to manage the events that follow. The *RISKMAN* risk management methodology comprises eight steps. Six of these form the essential risk management process and comprise identification, assessment, evaluation, mitigation, budget provisioning, monitoring and control.

During identification risks are classified, as shown earlier in Figure 2.6, under the twelve risk classes of strategic, marketing, contractual, financial, master plan, definition, process, product, organisation, operational, maintenance and external. These classes form the basis for operating the risk management process, and guide the allocation of ownership of individual risks to the most suitable persons in the organisation.

An essential and critical part of the risk process during the bid stage of a project, is risk mitigation where possible, followed by the development of the risk budget to provision risks that cannot be wholly mitigated. The risk budget is set after the estimating process is completed, including estimating the contingencies associated with each activity and subcontract, that has an associated risk. Using the risk contingency estimates, which may have set the initial price estimate at an unacceptable high level, *RISKMAN* assists and encourages higher management to make the necessary decisions to increase or decrease the risk exposure of the company by setting a risk budget, related to the perceived market conditions.

The seventh activity in *RISKMAN* is risk audits, whose purpose is to ensure that the risk management process is implemented throughout each stage in the project (contract) life cycle. Its usefulness is enhanced by its integration with the capturing of corporate experience for a professional risk-driven project management process, which is part of the eighth activity - ensuring continuous improvement in the management of risk.

The establishment of a project history file is essential to and used in the risk audit process. Its use must include the capture of corporate experience, by documenting the decision and financial history of the project and the reasons behind those decisions. When things have gone wrong the file can be used to determine why and when. When things have gone well, the effectiveness of the risk management process can be addressed, and the history file with its corporate experience is used to speed the audit process and to make recommendations for the future by summarising the experience in a project completion report.

The eight steps forming the essential process of RISKMAN cannot, of course be carried out in isolation from the business. Supporting elements are required, in terms of data and people management, in order to achieve results. These supporting elements, shown in Figure 3.1, surround the two processes at the heart of RISKMAN, namely the risk management process, and the risk-driven project management process, which form the subject of this chapter.

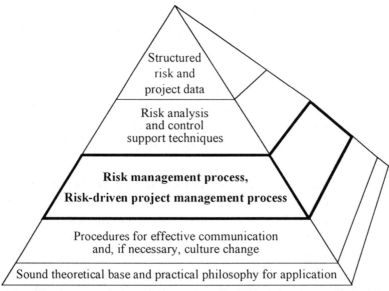

Figure 3.1 The five elements of the *RISKMAN* methodology.

3.1 *RISKMAN* management levels

In introducing risk management into a company, the *RISKMAN* methodology provides the ability to be selective in the level of risk management applied to meet the company needs and any demands for risk management imposed by the market.

Risk management must be a profitable activity as well as improving the maturity of project management. This can increase the likelihood of winning extra business, as the company demonstrates its maturity in project risk management.

Three *RISKMAN* application levels are defined within Chapter 6:

- **Basic** level *RISKMAN*
- **Intermediate** level *RISKMAN*
- **Comprehensive** level *RISKMAN*

Each of these application levels provide a complete risk management process. When moving from one level to a higher level, the degree of accuracy through analysis will be improved, but with a corresponding increase in the costs of the risk management process.

Some of the techniques in the comprehensive application level are best managed by persons with an extensive knowledge of the tools available and their application.

The intermediate application level requires a more intensive training in risk management skills, and a less exhaustive level of knowledge of the theory of probability.

3.2 The philosophy of *RISKMAN*

In this section we will see how a risk is described and managed throughout the *RISKMAN* methodology. Some concepts have been presented generally in Chapters 1 and 2 but need to be formalised in order to provide a coherent management core, leading to a common language inside an organisation.

3.2.1 Birth and life of a risk

A risk has a life which is the time period during which it may occur, starting with the event that triggers its inception, right through to the end of its effects on the programme or activities. This life-cycle is important to management because it enables risks to be anticipated and control to be implemented during the **active period.** The active period is represented by:

a set of dates: start date and end date

project phases: running between the project start date and the end date signified by project completion.

A risk has also a birth, which is the period during which a factor or combination of factors may lead to its existence. We will call it the **generation period** and characterise it by the same information as the active period. If the factors that will give rise to a risk can be identified, then the time period for management to take mitigation action can be bounded.

Active and generation periods can overlap, for example, a risk of paying penalties is generated at the contract negotiation phase, and may happen at the end of the project, during the delivery period.

3.2.2 Risk classes

The risk classification in Figure 2.6 identified twelve main headings under which risks may be grouped on projects. Of course, one could ask why such a complex classification is necessary. There are several reasons for this as follows:

- **risks need to be managed appropriately**: we will need specific identification, qualification, analysis and reduction techniques to be used by qualified people, with appropriate effort and accuracy.

- **risks need to have 'owners' responsible for their management:** of course, skills and responsibilities involved to achieve a project vary tremendously, and a risk must be monitored by someone who is as near as possible to its impact and controlled by people who are as near as possible to its causes and are best able to manage the risk. The analysis of roles and responsibilities will be addressed later.

- **risks must not be overlooked:** a complete classification leads to an efficient analysis.

- **risk management should be built into the company's know-how:** moreover, the classification is a basis for the organisation to optimise its risk management effort. Depending on the type of business, some classes will be of more importance than others.

3.2.3 Probability

A risk may be characterised by a probability law describing the likelihood of its occurrence and/or its impact value across the time encompassed by the active period.

Management requirements do not necessarily include a need to analyse a risk precisely. Risk analysis is expensive, sometimes useless and may be irrelevant. Depending on the need, three levels of analysis accuracy are defined:

- basic level: probability is assessed simply as low, medium or high

- intermediate level: probabilities are given values either in the range 0 to 1 or as a percentage
- comprehensive level: probabilities are described by specifying a distribution function (e.g. normal, beta, skewed, triangular, etc.) and its parameters.

RISKMAN Application level	Probability during the active period
basic level	low/medium/high
intermediate level	0-1 or 0-100%
comprehensive level	

Figure 3.2 Probabilities in relation to *RISKMAN* levels

It is very rare that high level analysis is needed. Generally this is required when complex and precise simulation (such as Monte Carlo) must be achieved, or for system behaviour and reliability calculations. Low to medium level analysis covers most management requirements adequately. The medium level is required when a risk has a long active period and uncertainty concerning its occurrence and/or impact increases during that time. Three levels of probability are identified as shown in Figure 3.3.

	Probability range
low	0 - 0.1
medium	0.1 - 0.3
high	0.3 - 1

Figure 3.3 Probability ranges for basic assessment

3.2.4 Impact

The impact of a risk should be measured according to any or all of the following units:

- Cost: any financial unit.
- Time: generally representing a delay in delivery or programme.

- Quality or Customer Requirements: represented by a lack of performance, or not meeting a specific technical constraint such as a level of reliability, etc.

These units are not exclusive one from the other. In the *RISKMAN* approach, a risk can impact the schedule and/or cost of a project, and/or can prevent deliveries or requirements being met, but not necessarily all of them at the same time. We will consider (Section 3.2.5) how they influence one another.

The product of the probability and the impact of a risk is the **risk exposure** which represents the expectation, if we look at the risk as a random variable. Intuitively, the risk exposure is the loss provision made for a risk if a sufficient number of situations where this risk can occur are analysed (e.g. aeroplane crashing near an airport).

Unfortunately, an isolated risk exposure value is not very interesting for a project because each project is a unique situation and the risk will either happen or not. However, the exposure value provides a convenient means to compare risks amongst themselves because as stated by most authors (Boehm, Charette, Chapman, etc.) comparing impacts or probabilities is meaningless.

As an example, let us consider two risks, with characteristics as shown in Figure 3.4.

	Probability	Impact
R1	0.0001	£1M
R2	0.5	£1,000

Figure 3.4　Example risks

A management procedure based on probability would be likely to exclude R1, even though the impact is extensive. However, if based on impact, then R2 would be likely to be excluded.

In terms of exposure $E(R1) = 100$ and $E(R2) = 500$. This is a close order of magnitude and therefore, even if opinions differ, both must be taken into account.

Degrees of risk exposure can be evaluated as follows:

Unacceptable risk: exposure to risks which can jeopardise company strategy and/or present dangers to human lives and/or represent a significant financial exposure.

Critical risk: exposure to risks which can injure achievement of company strategy, and/or cause significant material and human damage and/or represent a major financial exposure.

Significant risk: which can cause operation problems, but is budgetable.

Minor risk: which does not cause significant problems and represents a relatively small financial amount.

Area of concern: not yet significant in terms of risk as the causes involved have very low probability. Nevertheless they have potential impacts which might become significant, and therefore the probabilities should be kept under review.

	Low probability	Medium probability	High probability
High impact	Critical	Unacceptable	Unacceptable
Medium impact	Significant	Critical	Unacceptable
Low impact	Minor	Significant	Critical

Figure 3.5 Classes versus qualified risk impact and probability

3.2.5 Inaccuracy in probability and impact estimates

One of the more obvious difficulties with risk management is to ensure acceptable accurate evaluation of impact and probability when quantification is needed.

This is a major point for which two alternatives may be considered:

- provide an effective method for quantifying the risks
- work with rough estimates, but be aware that there is a level of uncertainty involved

The first alternative is certainly better, but may not be cost-effective when it is only necessary to know that an important risk exists, and that it needs to be mitigated. In other words, approximate evaluation may be perfectly acceptable in certain cases, as long as the uncertainty in the information is handled with care.

Two alternative solutions are available to estimate with adequate accuracy the probability of an event:

- Identify the combination of causes leading to that event. This is the fault tree, cause-effect diagram or decision tree approach.

- Observe a significant number of occurrences of the event in similar environmental conditions, i.e. other projects. This can only be achieved by gathering historical data.

In the case of impacts, there is no general rule except the fact that appropriate quantification techniques must be applied. Examples of useful techniques are presented in Appendix E. However, when a value is uncertain, it is always preferable to provide a range of possible outcomes (optimistic, probable, pessimistic) which may be associated with a scale value.

3.2.6 Causes, effects and consequences

In risk analysis, a situation can, most of the time, be characterised by a sequence of causes having effects and leading to an undesired consequence. Analysis of such situations has been enhanced by methods like fault-trees for example, used extensively in systems reliability evaluation.

Without appropriate terminology, most meetings at which discussions on risk take place turn out to be perfectly incoherent conversations, everyone dealing with causes, effects and consequences in a different way, and naming everything risk: "there is a risk, we do not have a marketing plan for this operation", "the customer is not able to define his need properly", "Jones will not have the time to look at the contractual terms carefully". Of course, this information, which is of tremendous value for a risk analysis, reflects everybody's know-how and expertise, but is not organised. Therefore, the *RISKMAN* methodology suggests a systematic approach. We will view them as the "*RISKMAN* rules".

First Rule: A risk must belong to one and only one classification, and its impact be measured (or evaluated) in one and only one unit.

The need for this rule has been commented upon in Section 2.1.7.

Second Rule: A risk may have one or several causes. A risk may give rise to one or more other risks, in other words, a situation may be characterised by networks of causes effects and consequences as shown in Figure 3.6. The causes may be facts or constraints (see Section 3.6.3). Effects and consequences are risks belonging to classes and measured according to a precise unit.

For management needs, and because the method is mainly for commercial environments, we distinguish between risks having a financial impact, and risks without direct financial impact (measured in time, features or quality).

The target is that at the end of a risk analysis, all risks with financial impact are detected. Therefore:

Third Rule: Every risk without direct financial impact must lead directly or indirectly to one or several risks with financial impact.

This means that everything will be turned into a cost in the end. Of course, things can be indirect and go through other risks without direct financial impact.

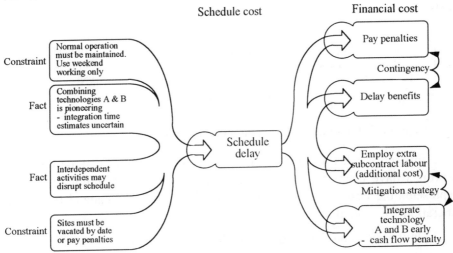

Figure 3.6 Cause and effect sequence in risk analysis

For example, a **schedule** risk of project delay may lead to four different risks as shown in Figure 3.6 with financial impact:

Contractual risk:	paying penalties.
Opportunity risk:	delaying benefits
Resource risk:	need to employ additional subcontract labour
Financial risk:	additional cash flow costs for early integration testing, to allow troubleshooting time later.

One might ask why these values could not be merged into only one risk. The answer is that most of the time these four risks will not have the same probabilities. In any event, some may occur and some may not.

The resource risk may have the same probability as the schedule risk, because if the schedule shifts, the team must still be paid.

The contractual risk may be manageable: customer negotiation, contingency in the contract. Therefore, its probability is clearly lower.

The financial risk: most companies, large and small, have means to manage them: advance payments, factoring, insurance, etc.

A schedule risk may be caused by another risk such as not meeting a requirement constraint measured in performance quality, or from the uncertainty in estimating accuracy (measured in time).

Now, to ensure a coherent analysis, we need the following rule:

Fourth Rule: Two risks with financial impact represent totally separate costs.

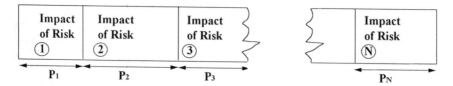

Figure 3.7 Cumulative financial impact of risks

With this set of rules, we ensure that once all risks with a financial impact on a project have been identified and quantified, their total cumulative impact represents the best estimate of the potential worst case financial loss on the operation. We avoid:

Omissions: non-detected risks with financial impact.

Overlaps: the same cost counted twice.

With the first level of analysis, the list of risks with financial impact represents a set of disjointed potential costs, each of them having their own probability of occurrence, as shown in Figure 3.7.

Event	Probability	Impact
Nothing	$P(1-P_1)*(1-Pn)$	Nothing
R_1	$P_1*(1-P_2).....*(1-Pn)$	I_1
R_2	$(1-P_2)*P_2*.....*(1-Pn)$	I_2
R_1 and $R_2.....Rn$	$P_1*P_2*.....*Pn$	$I_1+I_2+I_3+.....In$

Figure 3.8 Decision table for risk combinations

Therefore, if we can establish that the risks are independent from each other, we can produce a decision table describing all potential combinations, see Figure 3.8.

It is then possible to sort the events in the decision table by increasing impact value and to draw the curve of probability versus cumulative impact, to arrive at a maximum financial impact value for the project.

The curve shown in figure 3.9 represents the **project exposure to loss**, and is an example of a cumulative impact and probability curve on a project (assumes that $I(R1) < I(R2) < I(R3).......$).

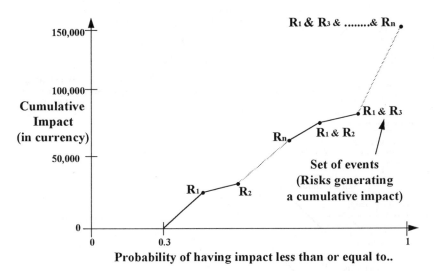

Figure 3.9 Cumulative impact/probability curve

If, however, some of the risks are not independent, and the occurrence of one risk is linked to the occurrence of another, then it becomes necessary to use a decision tree for the purpose of studying the combinations and their impact.

Concerning the causes, research and modelling can, in certain cases, be a very expensive operation, incompatible with the size of the programme and the amount of management effort. The reasons for this are now obvious: the amount of information on a programme may be very large; everything cannot be evaluated with accuracy (especially at the beginning); sequences of causes and effects may sometimes lead to the need for six or seven levels of analysis.

In most cases, one level is enough even though the model is then less accurate.

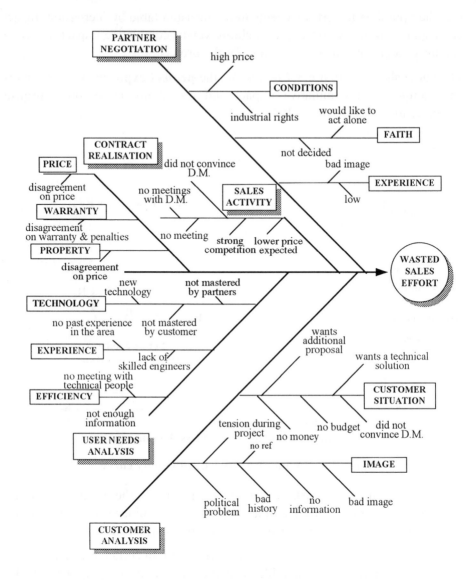

Figure 3.10 Example cause effect (Ishikawa) diagram

In order to preserve risk management cost-effectiveness, we identify three levels of identification from the most simple to the extremely sophisticated to be able to adapt the management effort.

Basic level: the causes of a risk are simply listed. This result can be obtained with simple checklists or cause effect diagrams such as is shown in Figure 3.10. One level of causes is then used.

Intermediate level: cause-effect diagrams or fault trees are established, including a hierarchy of causes organised with a first order logic (and/or relations, etc.). In this case the number of levels is not limited.

Comprehensive level: a network (model) is established which allows not only sequences of events, but also circuits. Most of the time reality proves that a chain of events lead to reinforcement of the events at the beginning of the chain. Two techniques are available for this, Markov chains and causal networks.

3.2.7 Triggers

A risk trigger is an event, which may be assigned by management, that initiates risk management activity to mitigate the potential effects of a risk occurring. It is the time event by which the project manager can state that a specific risk will be incurred if no action is taken. The management purpose is to minimise the impact of a risk, if possible by detecting it and taking action early.

As an example (refer to Figure 3.11) for a schedule risk the 45° diagram extrapolation curve goes beyond the contingency float: a risk may be incurred if the necessary resources manager requires 5-6 weeks to recruit staff, so a trigger event is set some 6 weeks prior to the risk, to ensure that the action is initiated.

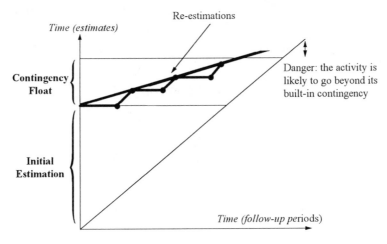

Figure 3.11 The 45° diagram

3.3 *RISKMAN* in the context of the business

There are four, and only four, fundamental functions at the core of any business. These are:

- Marketing activity - identifying, creating and satisfying demand from customers.

- Technical activity - research, development design and testing of new products, and quality assurance.

- Production and Operation activity - producing and delivering to the customer, products at the right price, quality and time.

- Financial and Accounting activity.

These functions must, of course, be driven in a sound strategic direction from the top by directors responsible to the business' funders. This is shown in Figure 3.12.

Figure 3.12 Fundamental view of a business

The mechanism by which strategic direction is implemented has to be by executing projects. Those projects can vary from research, through product development, to process development, the construction of new factories, facilities or offices, to training programmes and re-organisations, or marketing campaigns. So, the central function of providing strategic direction shown in Figure 3.12 can be replaced by project activity. This turns the fundamental view of the business into a process as shown in Figure 3.13.

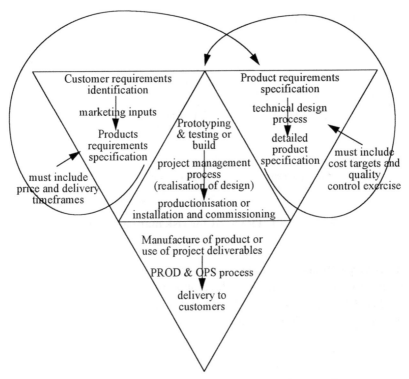

Figure 3.13 Process of business development and operation

Business ventures are fundamentally risk-taking activities to a greater or lesser extent. The relative size of the risk will determine the attention which must be given to risk management. This is illustrated in Figure 3.14.

Projects provide the link between marketing (high risk) and research and development (high risk) on the one hand and, on the other hand, operations - where large amounts of money are spent over long periods and so in this area risk must be reduced to a low level.

Projects are full of risk compared with the operations environment, but are relatively low risk when compared to technical research or marketing. Managed well, the project should be used to deliberately measure and take control of the risk that is inevitable in research and marketing so that only a minimum of uncertainty is passed on into the operating environment.

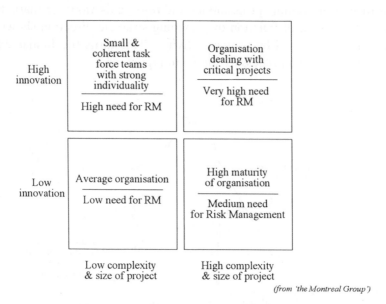

(from 'the Montreal Group')

Figure 3.14 The need for risk management

Project activity can also be viewed (see Figure 3.15) as the centre of an hour-glass which measures the gradual development of business activity over the years. *RISKMAN* is a structural and deliberate means to take control of individual projects within the business.

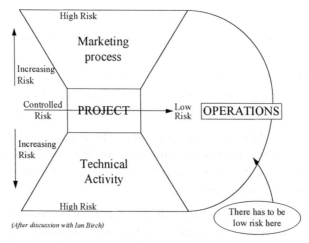

(After discussion with Ian Birch)

Figure 3.15 The place of *RISKMAN* in the business process

3.3.1 Processes and milestones

Depending on its profile and nature, a project requires co-ordination between several major concurrent processes in an organisation:

the strategic process: this is the high-level management analysis and planning for the company's position in its selected markets, its image, and financial targets. It is essential to involve this process level in decision making, to ensure that company resources are not committed adversely to projects and that the risks are properly considered when seeking project approval decisions.

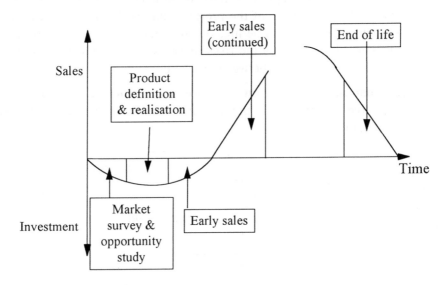

Figure 3.16 Marketing process

the marketing process: this is linked to lines of products/projects and to the activities necessary for management to take a position on a market, i.e. market analysis, investments for product realisation, sales force deployment, early sales and advertisements, maturity period and end of product life (see Figure 3.16). Of course, such activities may not be fully invoked when a supplier is contracted to realise and deliver a specific product or project to one customer. Whatever the situation, the risks within these activities and their effect on winning projects, must also be evaluated.

the contractual process: this represents the contractual activities between a customer and his supplier: bid, negotiation, contract execution, warranty period, maintenance, etc., (see Figure 3.17).

The contract clauses which modify the process and may form part of the specification form potential sources of risk, many of which may be the normal business risks.

the development process: activities that lead to a specific realisation of the project: needs (requirements) analysis, feasibility studies, definition, studies, design, production, test, deployment, project management, configuration management, quality, etc. (see Figure 3.18).

the production process: those activities involved in taking a developed item through to a finished marketable product. On some projects, the execution of the project requires the development and production processes to be linked and managed by the same project manager. This requires the risks to be evaluated, not only in each process, but within and between processes.

the customer support and maintenance process: this includes corrective maintenance, preventative maintenance and evolution maintenance.

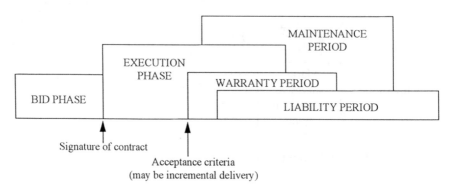

Figure 3.17 Contractual process

To manage the risks which could damage a programme, it is necessary to plan strategic and contractual decisions by following a step-by-step process. This process must be followed before each new release of project finances on a comparison between results of previous phases, expectations and evolution of previously identified risks, i.e. changes to the risk exposure either beneficial or adverse.

A means for co-ordination between the project processes involved is necessary to manage risks and this is normally provided by the project programme (schedule), managed by the project manager. The financial and other resources assigned must match with the tangible and controllable deliverables, available at the end of technical phases. To manage the costs involved, it is necessary to determine the real technical progress within each activity and to be aware of when risks are being approached and the action to be taken to mitigate the effects. It is also essential as part of the project management that there to be a commitment to project review at key periods to get a clear picture of the status of the programme and to take necessary decisions in a timely fashion. At these meetings risk status must be included and any new risks discussed in an open environment.

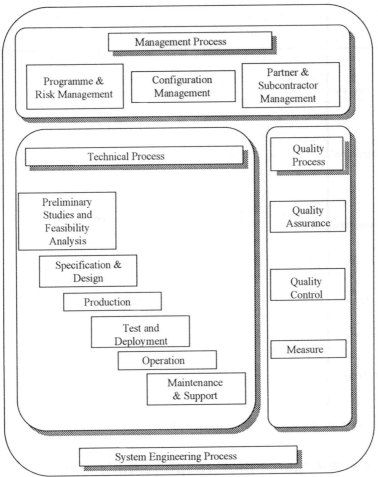

Figure 3.18 Development process

Specifically, the method is to identify critical phases and related milestones and meetings for key people to get adequate information to decide on budget release, work continuation, further investments, etc.

During these meetings, several scenarios and the risks within each should be evaluated in order to identify the best possible solution, optimising such parameters as costs, schedules, level of delivery, operational and quality constraints.

Each team on a project must manage a risk plan at its own level, which must form a part of a project risk master plan. Figure 3.19 shows a typical master plan describing the main milestones and specifying their pilot process. These milestones are sequential.

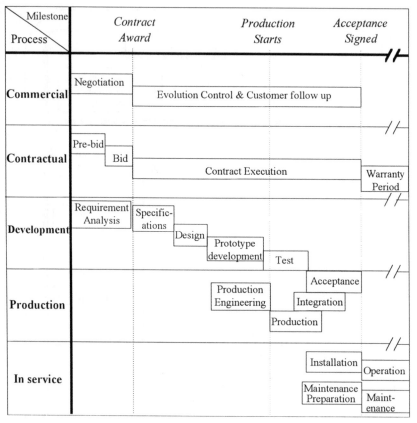

Figure 3.19 Typical project master plan

3.3.2 Extra-organisation responsibility levels

The following classification is defined for different people involved in a programme:

- extra-organisation responsibility level;
- intra-organisation responsibility level.

Extra-organisation responsibility levels are the standard responsibility levels assumed by different organisations involved in a common operation (programme). Three levels can be identified:

- the purchaser,
- the prime contractor,
- the subcontractor.

Each company normally nominates a programme manager to assume an appropriate level of responsibility as its official representative. However, in the case of a product development based on internal investments, the three levels may be assumed by managers of the same company, but from different departments.

Purchasers generally work for end users or for themselves. They are responsible for the technical requirements specification of the system, place the order for the system development and track progress. They permanently act as user representatives and control the budget.

Specifically, their expertise must focus on the following areas:

identify needs and pre-design the system to organise its realisation;

choose the prime contractor and the main partners;

establish the budget and the delivery dates for the system;

negotiate the warranties;

define the quality objectives including performance and acceptance levels;

manage the implementation including acceptance of the project;

monitor and report on programme status.

The purchasers therefore assume an important role in the procurement process particularly during phases of technical definition (system specification and design) and of system validation and acceptance. Purchasers generally pass the major risks of implementation down to prime contractors for managing. However, purchasers are themselves sources of risk.

Prime contractors work for purchasers. They must assume responsibility for the design and control of the system. They are responsible for the system development and test from specification through production, installation, integration and acceptance.

They must execute the following tasks:

identify requirements and develop the detailed specifications;

check for system feasibility;

estimate costs, effort and schedule;

forecast the budgets in accordance with payment milestones;

choose subcontractors and partners;

build the implementation team;

provide the programme management;

prepare the integration phase and manage the programme through each of its implementation phases.

The prime contractor, therefore plays a major role in the procurement process during the phases of technical definition (system specification and design), of system integration and of system validation and acceptance. By definition, the prime contractor is therefore the major risk owner in a project.

Subcontractors are prime contractors for a part of the system (sub-system or equipment). In their turn, they can commission other subcontractors (minor subcontractors or suppliers). Therefore, they assume a prominent role in the procurement process subject to the system and skills for which they are responsible. The subcontractor is a major mitigator and therefore manager of risk.

3.3.3 Intra-organisation responsibility levels

Functional skills are required inside an organisation to implement the processes identified in Section 3.3.1.

Marketing process: a product/sales (marketing) manager.

Contractual process: a legal adviser for contractual aspects and a commercial manager for selling aspects.

Programme management process: project manager, responsible for overall management of the project related to the realisation of the whole system.

Finance manager: a manager who maintains project financial status for the project manager, and releases funds for risk contingency when authorised.

Procurement manager: a manager who places contracts with suppliers of systems and services.

Technical process: typically in accordance with the sub-processes:

functional managers (team leaders), responsible for technical management of sub-projects, related to the realisation of systems and/or sub-systems;

configuration manager for the whole system;

support manager responsible for the logistics and in-service support of the system, and equipment;

quality manager who ensures quality of the system and of its realisation;

operations manager, where the product (project) is to be operationally controlled;

risk manager (unless the function is assumed within the project manager's responsibilities).

3.4 The risk management process

As we have seen, the risk management process is a distinct process embedded within the larger schema of the risk-driven project management process.

The risk management process is a cyclical process which can be likened to the second hand on a stopwatch, in that it goes around many times as the project proceeds (see Figure 3.20).

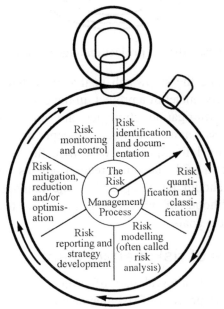

Figure 3.20 The risk management process is a repetitive cycle

In a similar manner, the risk-driven project management process can be likened to the minute hand, representing a sequence of stages which runs its course just once through the life-cycle of the project, shown in Figure 3.21.

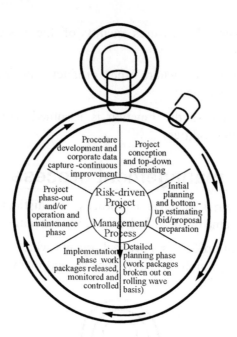

Figure 3.21 The risk-driven project management process

Real project life is like the stopwatch in that it is dynamic and continually moving. From the very outset of a project, in the conception phase, as soon as a risk is identified, mitigation strategies are considered as part of the quantification process, and a project concept developed in which no unacceptable risks are left exposed - otherwise the whole thing ends right there.   Each time a risk become recognised as significant, the risk management cycle should be completed if the management team wish to maximise the likelihood of proceeding smoothly towards a successful achievement of project goals.

3.4.1 The steps of risk management

Risk management is an integral part of project management.   It is not a separate activity. The process of risk management has to be integrated with the project management process and this is what the *RISKMAN* methodology does.

The risk activity breakdown is shown in Figure 3.22.   These activities comprise a number of steps, each of which have to be addressed by the company's functional and project managers, to successfully implement risk management; they are briefly described below.

Figure 3.22 Risk management activities

Risk analysis: the work involved in identifying and evaluating a risk.

Identification: the work involved in identifying the potential risks to the successful completion of a business, project, or work activity, including classifying and recording each risk, qualifying the risk by reaching a unique description of the risk element, estimating its probability (likelihood) of occurrence and potential impact on the programme in terms of timescales, costs or quality (performance).

The process also includes the identification of the person, team or company that will be responsible for managing the risk out (i.e. the risk owner), and the recording of the existence of the potential risk in a manner that enables it to be open to scrutiny, by its insertion into an appropriate classification.

Risk evaluation: the work involved in modelling the programme, conducting a sensitivity analysis and prioritising the risks. Analysis is an essential part of the evaluation activity, enabling the exposure within delivery timescales and costs to be quantified.

Risk control: the work involved in the monitoring and reporting to higher management of the status of the risks and the effectiveness of the mitigation strategies. It also includes the provision of the means by which higher management can monitor that risk management is being implemented and that when things appear to be going wrong, can verify that risk management is being effectively applied.

Mitigation strategies are planned and means devised by which the impact of the risk may be reduced, its occurrence prevented, the risk avoided, or the need for contingencies to be put in place to compensate for the risk should it occur, determined.

During project execution, risk mitigation is aimed at the implementation of the previously identified mitigation strategy.

Risk control also includes the estimation and calculation of the risk exposure, in financial terms, caused by the impact of the risk on the programme, with due consideration of the moderating effect of the mitigation strategy.

An amount of money is calculated and allocated to each risk element, and the sum of the money forms the risk contingency fund. A key factor in arriving at the contingency to be included in the cost estimates is ensuring that the price to the customer remains competitive.

To prevent over-estimation of the risk contingency, the contingency included within the subcontractor's prices must also be taken into account, and there must be no hidden subsidies within any of the cost estimates. In the decision process, higher management is informed of the risk involved in a project and their acceptance and approval to the risk exposure is sought.

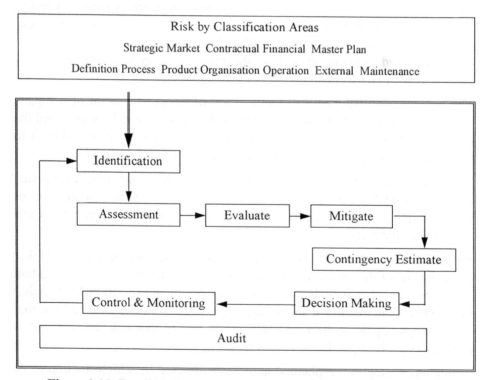

Figure 3.23 Detailed diagram of management cycle

Continual improvement: the work involved in training of project personnel in the latest techniques and best practices of risk management, and in the analysis of the corporate data within the project history file to extract the lessons learned for future projects.

The above activities are not set in concrete; they may be adjusted to meet the appropriate application level of *RISKMAN* (Basic, Intermediate, Comprehensive) as explained in Section 3.1.

The risk activities can be shaped into a risk management process as shown in Figure 3.23. This process is integrated into the company procedures and specifically the project management procedures for each functional area of the organisation.

Fig. 3.3.2(a) Risk budgeting /Version 1/25-08-93

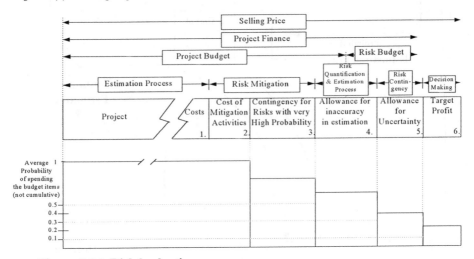

Figure 3.24   Risk budgeting

3.4.2 Risk budgeting

A key factor in the risk management process is the work involved in arriving at the risk contingency fund to be included within the final price within a proposal to a customer.

This risk budgeting activity is applicable at both intermediate and comprehensive levels of treatment, as it involves quantification.

The estimated price for the work involved in a project will be formed by the estimators, essentially from six prime cost elements as shown in Figure 3.24, each having a decreasing probability of being disbursed. The relative size of the boxes shown in Figure 3.24 is NOT intended to indicate the recommended relative proportions of the constituents that make up the budget. It has been

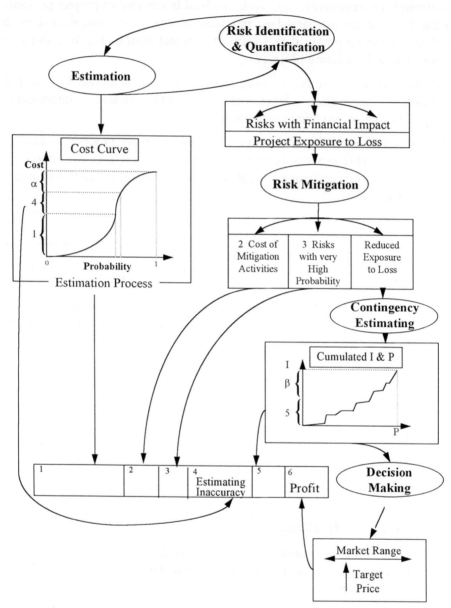

Figure 3.25 Process of establishing the risk budget

advocated that items 3, 4 and 5 are likely to amount to less than 10% of the budget, whilst, hopefully, item 6 alone represents a similar proportion.

Project costs (1): which includes raw costs for manpower, materials expenses and recoverable overheads. The project costs are evaluated with appropriate financial models during the estimation process, and is based on the resource estimates submitted by functional work areas.

Cost of risk mitigation strategies (2):   where the work would form a significant element of the project, e.g. a parallel path for a risky development activity or an insurance cost, it is formed from any cost that must be expended as a direct cost for mitigating the risks irrespective of whether the risk will be incurred.

Contingency for risks with very high probability of occurrence (3): e.g. more than 50%. These are risks with financial impact. Their total impact, however mitigated, is budgeted for here.

Allowance for inaccuracy in estimates (4): the causes of poor estimates are numerous: badly expressed needs, inappropriate estimate models, vague data, lack of history. Therefore, in some cases, it proves itself necessary to build a contingency to cope against excessive optimism. Note that the larger the database of information from comparable projects and the use of stringent guidelines to functional department estimators on the variances that should be allowed for within their estimates, the less is the need for this prime cost element.

Uncertainty allowance (5): this comprises the risk contingency costs, initially arrived at by the estimators, taking into account the residual risks and the calculated risk contingency for identified risks.

Target profit (6): the maximum level of profit that is assigned by the company for the type of project.

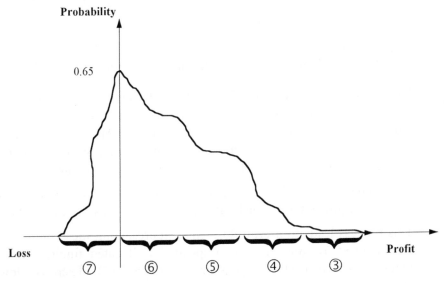

Figure 3.26 Profit and loss curve

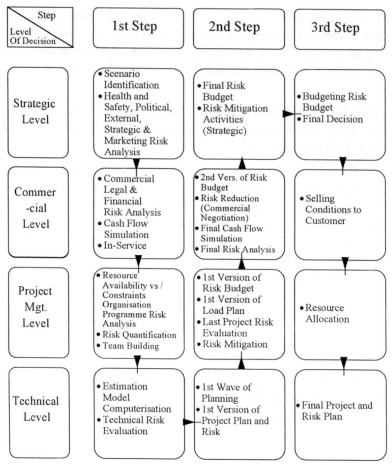

Figure 3.27 Step-by-step Approach to Project and Risk Budgets

The steps shown in Figure 3.25 illustrate the process of getting the budget together. As can be seen in the cost curve, there is an element α which represents that part of the estimating risk for which no allowance has been made, or, in other words, the amount by which the allowance (4) falls short of that necessary to fully cover for the pessimistic cost estimate.

In a similar fashion, the uncertainty allowance (5) is chosen at a point which is felt to be prudent, but which falls short of that necessary for total coverage.

This process leads to a profit/loss curve representing these numbers and the likelihood of avoiding having to spend the allocated funds. As shown in Figure 3.24 some costs are spent anyway (1) and (2). There is a low chance of not spending item (3), better chances of not incurring item (4), (5) is real security, and spending item (6) is bad luck (or bad management).

Item (7) is the potential for loss, and is represented by $(\alpha) + (\beta) - (6)$ (see Figure 3.25). This assumes, of course, that the evaluations are correct or at least significant. It is a target, not reality. Risk control and monitoring will provide mechanisms to check whether the analysis was done with appropriate accuracy.

The process of putting the budget together is done in several steps according to management level as shown in Figure 3.27, each management level only having a limited approval authority. Whilst the above budget may be included by the project management team in arriving at the price for a project, the decision-making process may adjust the price upwards to decrease the exposure, or downwards to win, but increasing the exposure.

3.4.3 The estimate, the bid, and the contract

When the estimated price is calculated, that price would normally be evaluated against the market expectation for the type of project or product, i.e. the risks of losing or winning the bid must be evaluated.

This price is presented for approval to higher management, together with any recommendations for changes (normally reductions) to make the offer attractive within the market.

The options open to higher management are to accept the price as estimated, increase the price to account for their perceptions of the risk or market worth, or to reduce the price to make the offer more acceptable.

The decision taken by higher management will, therefore, either reduce or increase the risk exposure of the company. If the decision is to reduce risk exposure by increasing the price, then the chances of winning in the market will also be reduced, or if the project is won, then higher than anticipated profits may be realised.

Should the decision be taken to increase the risk exposure, then if the project is won the project manager may find himself in the untenable situation of managing a project with insufficient funding in place to account for the risks within the project.

A major part of the risk management process is the maximisation of the benefit to the company by improving the management of risks, and reduction of the spending of risk contingency to improve profit.

The risk budget, i.e. the final risk contingency included within the price offered to the market will therefore be defined by the decisions taken by higher management concerning the acceptable level of risk exposure.

A reduced budget for risk within the offer price may be further reduced during negotiations, and if the specification remains unchanged, the budget may be insufficient to cover the risks.

This requires that risk contingency budgets for the individual risks be re-evaluated during contract start-up and/or adequate provisions be made by higher management to provide financial cover for the risks should they arise.

3.5 Core of the *RISKMAN* approach

3.5.1 Risk-driven project management

As we have seen previously, the risk management process cannot be totally separated from the project management process. Each activity feeds the other by providing critical information:

- estimates cannot be made accurately without the quantified risks;
- proper risk identification cannot be achieved without the project breakdown structure.

Therefore, risk management is useful for modelling the inaccuracy inherent to project management. It admits that the *exact* behaviour of a project cannot be forecast, and it addresses this shortcoming by identifying the major options and the way open to manage them for the best result.

The purpose of this section is to present the natural flow of combined risk and project management activities.

We identify four major risk-driven project management activities which encapsulate detailed activities: analyse, estimate, organise and follow-up.

Figure 3.28 presents the overall flow of these major activities, the arrows representing the information exchange between them.

It is important to notice that the cycle of activities is repeating itself during the project, at different milestones. Each step (pre-bid, bid, implementation) represents a greater level of detail:

- analyse: more and more information on the requirements and the technical solution foreseen. This leads to definite breakdown structures after several steps (obviously the PBS cannot be identified before the technical solution), and therefore good risk identification (see Section 3.6).

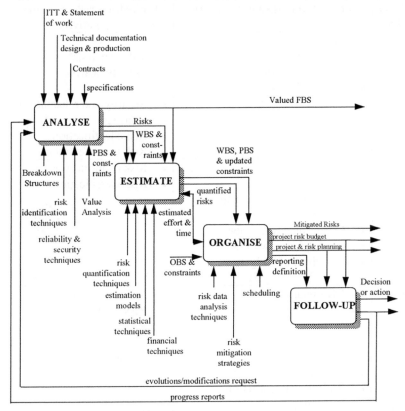

Figure 3.28 Risk-driven project management process

- estimate: greater accuracy based on a better idea of the needs, but also more accurate models. Cost breakdown is better than using a regression model. This leads to good and detailed risk analysis.

- organise: knowing precisely which resources are involved and scheduling the plan is a target definitely achieved only when the technical solution is identified, and also the test and installation strategy. Here again a rolling wave approach is necessary.

- follow-up: an activity that runs from the beginning to the end of a project.

Figure 3.29 identifies the detailed project managed and embedded risk management activities that relate to each major high level activity and shows how project and risk management activities may combine, and the sequence in which they do so.

High level activity	Project management activity	Embedded risk management activity
Analyse	• Needs analysis • FBS realisation • WBS realisation • PBS realisation	• Value analysis* • Activity analysis • Security and reliability study* • Constraint analysis* • Risk identification • Risk documentation
Estimate	• Time, cost and raw materials estimation • Master plan realisation • Consolidation with risks • First draft of budget • Cash flow analysis	• Risk quantification • Risk classification

Organise	• OBS realisation
	
	• Scheduling
	• Project plan realisation
	• Budgeting
	
	• Reporting definition
		• Risk ownership
		• Risk data analysis*
		• Risk mitigation
		  - strategies
		  - planning
		
		• Risk budgeting
		• Decision-making

Follow-up	• Monitoring indicators defined • Progress control • Evolution and change control • Reporting	• Risk reporting

* optional activities

Figure 3.29 Combination of project and risk management activities

3.6 Constraint analysis

A constraint is a specific characteristic imposed on a project or the product, either by the client (to meet his needs) or the designer (to find an adequate technical solution). In fact, managing a project involves meeting a series of constraints, i.e. the scheduling activity is a way of finding a solution (a PERT model) towards meeting several types of constraints such as resource availability, delivery dates, activity sequence and duration.

Of course, constraints have influence amongst themselves. Anyone having faced a project cost estimation exercise, knows how technical performance can postpone a delivery date, how a manufacturing constraint imposes a specific technology used in the design, etc.

Constraints are not always easy to meet. Therefore they can be the cause of risks. This is why constraint analysis is one of the major risk identification techniques. There are several objectives:

- identify the constraints generated by the requirements and directives in the baseline definition,
- document the project organisation and the technical solution through an appropriate model,
- trace the main constraints and identify secondary ones issued from the technical baseline,
- chase risks by analysing in which areas there is a significant likelihood of failing to overcome major constraints.

3.6.1 Customer baseline constraints

During the bid and negotiation process, the customer and his prime contractor will try to find the most acceptable compromise between, on the one hand the desire to be as close as possible to expectation (or even to exceed it) for the best price and the shortest schedule, and on the other hand ensuring the solution is feasible and can yield a decent profit. The ideal world would lead a vendor or a project manager to commit to what is reasonable. Unfortunately, this does not take account of the old story about "getting the business". Fierce competition tends to make offers less realistic. In other words, customers believe they will benefit from extremely attractive offers at low prices, but in the long run they may have to pay a high price for it.

Whatever the business climate is, constraint analysis is a useful exercise, especially before an important negotiation. Too many commitments are made without detailed analysis of their technical and ultimate cost implications.

This is what constraint analysis, combined with risk management, is intended to provide.

The basis for customer baseline constraint analysis is the set of information contained in such documents as:

the request for proposal (invitation to tender);

the requirements analysis (needs analysis);

the contract (or bid) (proposal and contract documentation);

the master plan (programme, schedule).

These documents along with additional details on the project will, by their nature, impose constraints on:

delivery dates of product;

operational requirements and quality;

implemented functions;

costs.

3.6.2 Project modelling

The project manager will normally represent the project by using well-established techniques (breakdown structures) on which additional information is provided:

The first model that is created is a Functional Breakdown Structure (FBS) which is a tree representing all the product functions, and for each of them their decomposition into sub-functions. Each function is linked to its set of constraints.

Secondly, the process and activities are represented by a Work Breakdown Structure (WBS), plus constraints on activities such as sequence, requested timing, resource profile, technical characteristics and interfaces.

Thirdly, the team view is represented by an Organisational Breakdown Structure (OBS) plus resource availability, skill description, etc.

A step-by-step approach to the production of the breakdown structure must be adopted. These breakdowns can then be related to their associated activities in time sequence to the programme of deliverables. At this stage, the risks to achievement of the activities and hence the programme, can be easily identified by the participants by tracing the constraints.

3.6.3 Tracing the constraints

This activity consists of analysing the constraints expressed in the definition baseline and translating them into concrete constraints related to the functioning process, the system architecture and/or the organisation required to achieve them.

Definition baseline constraints can be expressed informally in a very general way, and can turn out to generate several constraints at the detailed description level of the project. For example, a functional execution performance need will lead to a reflection of this performance in several hardware components, may impose software development skill levels, and perhaps generate manufacturing constraints and even, for example, set temperature restrictions inside the body of a system.

Depending on the view, constraint tracing is done during the specific project modelling activities:

- Product Breakdown Structure (PBS): from needs analysis to architecture definition or design,

- Functional Breakdown Structure (FBS): from needs analysis to architecture definition or design,

View Breakdown Structure	Constraint Classes	Description/examples
PBS	Functional	Trace functions accomplished by sub-system/component.
	Environmental	Temperature, vibrations, weather conditions.
	Behavioural	Performance, resistance, fault tolerance, reliability, quality, etc.
	Characteristics	Type of technology/material shape, accessibility, change during operation.
	Interfaces	Physical, logical, protocols.
	Manufacturing	Industrialisation, assembling, environment, integration.
	Management	Cost, availability.
WBS	Sequential	Preceding and following tasks.
	Timing	Start and end date.
	Skills required (or resource characteristic if not human)	Resource profile, constraint erased when project scheduled.
OBS	Availability	Depends on commitments to other project and activities.
	Skills	Skill classification inside organisation
	Links with activities	Imposed by the project manager

Figure 3.30 Classification of constraints

- Work Breakdown Structure (WBS): from early stage planning to detailed scheduling,

- Organisation Breakdown Structure (OBS): during the various stages of project organisation, and during scheduling.

Not all constraints come from the definition baseline. Some of them will find their origin in the choices that are made by the project team for its organisation or technical solutions. For example, scheduling a project with an imposed latest end date, means that the scheduling algorithm will, itself, generate constraints on start or end dates which are not directly imposed by the major constraint, but by the solution the algorithm has elaborated. Of course, in such case, a float is likely to appear imposed by the specified end date being later than the self-imposed end date used in the algorithm.

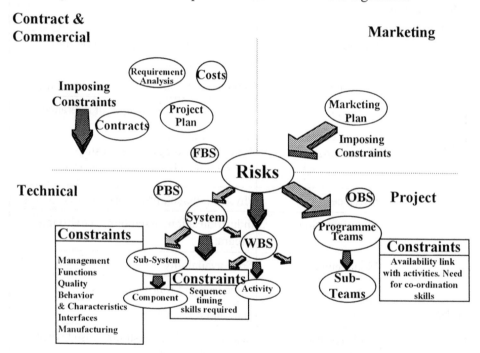

Figure 3.31 Constraints traceability

The origin of a constraint is a key element. Three types of constraints are defined:

- main constraints: originated from the definition baseline;

- secondary constraints: imposed by technical or organisational choices;

- minor constraints: imposed by a prior decision or because a choice is necessary.

In *RISKMAN*, we propose a classification of constraints related to each view. Figure 3.30 identifies classes and presents examples.

Figure 3.31 summarises the constraint-tracing process and shows how external factors such as marketing that are not directly related to the project (product) in hand, or to the FBS, PBS imposed by the customer's requirements, must be taken into consideration.

In a breakdown structure, each level has the same classes and types of constraints.

3.6.4 Constraints Identification

On a project, a significant part of the risk will exist because the possibility exists of not meeting a constraint because of things such as:

- tight schedule;
- performance on the edge of technology;
- operating environment too severe;
- etc.

Therefore, in the *RISKMAN* methodology constraints are considered to be causes of risk.

In most organisations using CPA or PERT, WBS and OBS, constraints are usually adequately managed. In the case of the FBS, the situation is different. Some standards impose tracing the constraints throughout performance allocation, or similar activities.

It is obvious that such an exercise may be expensive on a wide-ranging project, if one wants to make a complete analysis. This is why the *RISKMAN* methodology recommends at least a focus on constraints which are likely not to be met, i.e. the constraints leading to risks.

The constraint potentially leading to a risk will be analysed in terms of:

- a target: the goal to achieve on a project;
- reality: estimated or observed.

Target and reality are both analysed according to several criteria that are critical to the success of the activity:

- uncertainty: the ability to identify precisely or not, the constraint value or nature;
- ability to modify: to what extent the value and nature of the constraint can be changed;

```
┌─────────────────────────────────────────────────────────────────────┐
│ Project:                        Responsibility:                     │
│ Constraint Reference:              Type (1/2/3):                     │
│ PBS Code (1):            OBS Code (1):           WBS Code (1):       │
│                                                                     │
│ (1) mutually exclusive fields                                       │
└─────────────────────────────────────────────────────────────────────┘
```

```
┌─────────────────────────────────────────────────────────────────────┐
│ Class (2) :                                                         │
│ Description :                                                       │
│                                                                     │
│                                                                     │
└─────────────────────────────────────────────────────────────────────┘
```

```
┌─────────────────────────────────────────────────────────────────────┐
│ Is generated by (3) :                                               │
│ Generates (3) (4) :                                                 │
│                                                                     │
│ (3) constraint reference                                            │
└─────────────────────────────────────────────────────────────────────┘
```

Constraint Analysis

(4) if required, describe by probability model

(3) in percentage

	Uncertainty	Ability to modify	Dispersion	Cost
Target	(4)	(5)		
Reality	(4)	(5)	(6)	

Summary | H | L | H |H| Worst Case ──────────▶ Best Case | L | H | L | L |
          | H | L | | | | L | H | | |

```
┌─────────────────────────────────────────────────────────────────────┐
│ Risk Summary :                                                      │
│                                                                     │
│ Risk Reference :                                                    │
│                                                                     │
│                                                                     │
│                                                                     │
└─────────────────────────────────────────────────────────────────────┘
```

Figure 3.32 Constraint analysis sheet

- cost,
- dispersion between target and reality.

For example, risky situations can occur when one or several of the following circumstances happen to exist:

high uncertainty concerning the target,

uncertainty concerning estimated reality, with doubts about meeting the target (dispersion),

unchangeable target and doubts about meeting it (dispersion),

unchangeable reality outside the target (dispersion).

A constraint analysis sheet is presented in Figure 3.32 which summarises this concept. The result of the analysis will open to scrutiny, the potential risk mitigation strategies (see Section 4.4) for the constraint.

The illustration in figure 3.33 provides an example of how dispersion caused by unchangeable specifications (targets) and doubts about meeting the requirements can be analysed.

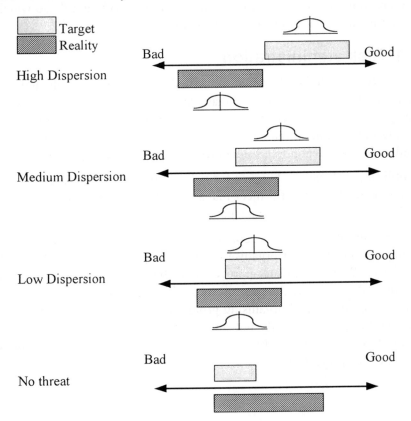

Figure 3.33 Dispersion analysis

3.7 Techniques

The application of techniques to the analysis and management of risk depends upon the complexity of the project, the propensity of the project to be significantly affected by risk, and the aspect of the project which is to be addressed. Projects which may be described as simple and less risk-prone can be managed, in respect to risk, using rudimentary techniques for the identification and evaluation of risk. At fairly mature stages of a project's realisation, when data is more prolific and the need more apparent, it may be advantageous to employ sophisticated risk scheduling techniques.

This section identifies the various techniques which can be used to address specific risk management functions and assesses the value, in terms of cost, accuracy and benefit, of employing them. Descriptions of specific risk modelling techniques are given in Appendix C.

Techniques for risk analysis and management can be partitioned into those which are more applicable to the *administration of risk*, and those which are more definable as *risk engineering techniques.*

3.7.1 Risk administration

Project risks need to be identified, classified, organised and evaluated, so that strategies can be formulated to mitigate, and therefore *manage the risk aspect of the project*. Certain techniques exist which will minister to this need and are more organisational than analytical in nature. Such techniques would be considered to be integral to a sound project management approach.

The utilisation of such techniques for risk administration purposes means that the employment of sound project management practices creates an excellent foundation for effective risk management.

Many organisations now adopt a Work Breakdown Structure (WBS) technique to identify and organise the work required to realise the project's objectives. Whilst such an approach may be considered only in terms of planning and controlling the project, we shall see that such a technique is also useful in identifying and organising project risks. If used in this fashion, the WBS can be used to classify not only all the work necessary to complete a given task, but also all the things which may adversely affect the conduct of that work - the project risks.

3.7.2 Risk engineering

The most recognisable techniques for risk analysis would be better described as risk engineering techniques. They include numerical analysis methods which whilst not designed specifically for risk analysis, are easily adaptable, and supremely suitable, for this purpose. In addition, techniques have been developed to specifically address certain aspects of project risk analysis. Principal amongst these are the techniques, and supporting systems, which have been produced to generate risk-driven project schedules. Examples are given in Appendix C.

The majority of numerical analysis methods for risk analysis would require the support of risk administration techniques to produce a coherent analytical model for risk management. On the other hand many of the specially developed schedule and budget risk analysis systems produce a definitive solution to a specific situation, and do not depend upon the support of any administrative facilities, thereby weakening the potential for effective risk management. It is infinitely better to embrace such formalised schedule risk analysis techniques within a structured risk administration method.

Activity	Development		Quality Control	Management		Risk Analysis	
Utility level	Needs and function analysis	Reliability design to cost		Estimating	Planning	Identification	Quantification
Basic	Function breakdown structures	Preliminary danger analysis Failure modes (FMECA)	Measures	Regression analysis models Parametric estimating	GANTT High-level plans	Check lists Ishikawa diagrams (cause-effect)	Probability and impact qualification Ranking Ownership
Inter-mediate	Value analysis Utility curves	Fault trees	FCM approach	Work breakdown structures	Critical path analysis PERT	Fault trees	Cost Breakdown Structure Impact estimation (one value)
Compre-hensive	Prototype building	Markov chains	Statistical analysis	Product Breakdown Structure	Monte Carlo simulation Controlled Interval and Memory	Influence networks Markov chains	Decision trees Impact estimation (3 values)

Figure 3.34 Table of techniques related to function

3.7.3 Levels to employ

The decision whether to employ a particular technique or not, is not immediately obvious. The fact that there may be uncertainty about the scheduling of a project may lead one to believe that a scheduling system, which has been designed to address that specific situation, should be used. This may dissipate any uncertainty concerning the schedule objectives, but create an unsustainable, and unnecessary, cost burden upon the management budget for the project.

As with most things, one needs to consider the cost and benefit aspects of such a decision. This requires more than a little thought because the potential cost of employing a technique may not be apparent; for example the use of a decision tree to formulate a mitigation strategy may not require any investment in costly computer support, but may absorb significantly high levels of man-time to create and analyse.

In Figure 3.34 techniques are mapped against risk analysis and management functions; and partitioned according to their utility level, which is a function of their perceived cost and accuracy. This does not impose a judgement upon the relative value of a technique, for instance a technique which is classed as being of low utility level, because it is relatively cheap to employ and less accurate than other techniques, may be a very valuable aid in fulfilling a particular function. This partition into utility levels is also imprecise in that some organisations may find it relatively inexpensive to employ a technique which has been classified as a comprehensive utility level.

When considering a technique to be employed one should take account of its value at a specific phase of the project. For instance one would rarely employ the technique of prototype building, to assess risk, prior to contract award, unless that particular activity was to be funded by the client. On the other hand, one would consider building a prototype during the development phase of the project - particularly if such an eventuality had been evaluated during the bidding process, and adequate funding generated in the risk budget.

The prudent, and least risk prone, approach would be to consider low utility level techniques before having to resort to more costly options. Adequate results may be obtained from fairly simple approaches to risk analysis, and one often finds that the maximum benefit is gained from those techniques which have been described as risk administration measures such as might be based on the sample risk analysis sheet shown in Figure 3.35. This does not denigrate the analytical procedures, which are extremely valuable when such an approach is necessary.

Risk Analysis Sheet

Project : _____   Responsibilities:_____
Risk Reference: _____   Generation period:_____
Class: _____ Active Period:_____

Description:

(1) Process & Life Cycle Phases   (2) Owner   (3) Responsible for Management

Exposure: _____

Very high			Cost	
High			Time	
Medium			Requirement	
Low				
Probability			**Impact unit & Value**	**Impact Description**

Causes	Effects

Description of Triggers

Trigger 1   Trigger 2   Trigger 3   Trigger 4

Mitigation Strategy

Contingency
Back-up plan
Insurance
Avoidance
Transference
Early Control
Buy Information

Description

Figure 3.35 Sample Risk Analysis Sheet

4
Operating The Risk Management Process

In this chapter an introduction is provided to the *RISKMAN* Risk Management Methodology operating process. The eight stages of the risk management processes shown in Figure 3.23 are described in detail, with emphasis in the areas of risk identification and mitigation. Risk identification is a most important aspect of risk management, because without reliable identification of significant risks the benefits are difficult to obtain. The concept of 'ownership' of risks and their consequences is also established.

The recognised methods for identifying risks, and their recording under the *RISKMAN* twelve major classes of risk, are described, and the need is established for these to relate to the management style and culture of the organisation, and to be linked into the cost identification process via the project Work Breakdown Structure (WBS).

Associated with risk identification is the initial risk quantification process, where the risks have an appropriate probability of occurrence and impact assigned and related to time, performance and cost, based on intuition and experience. These initial values are subjective assessments. Subsequent processing may refine these assessments and combine them with other uncertainties within a model to quantify the costs and timescales exposure. Using the initial estimates, the risks are evaluated and prioritised. Mitigation strategies are defined only for those risks with significant likelihood of occurrence and impact as to warrant a mitigation strategy.

Mitigation is described as a process with several categories; each category may be considered as being appropriate for particular forms of risk. The categories described are avoidance, transference, reducible, manageable and contingency (residual) risks. The mitigation categories are related to the appropriate stage in the project life cycle: pre-bid, bid, implementation and operation/phase-out stages.

An introduction to the subsequent processing and presentation of risk data is provided. This includes the storage and manipulation of risk information in databases and spreadsheets, and the linking of these to the project programme and project/cost database to provide management information.

In risk monitoring, operation and control, the management of risks in the database and of new risks as they arise is discussed. Successful risk management is dependent during implementation on having good project reporting procedures that enables management to determine the status of the project and, in particular, the finances of the project in relation to the outstanding risk occurrences that it may yet face.

The capturing of corporate experience is expanded with particular emphasis on the recording of reasons for decisions. The use of the project history file and the production of project completion reports to enable the benefits of experience to be obtained are both described.

The *RISKMAN* project risk management methodology requires the introduction not only of new procedures, but also of new forms for reporting of the risks and their management. Every effort has been made to keep these forms within the range of standard project management forms. Samples of some standard forms and a brief description of each and its use are provided. However, some forms are likely to need tailoring for any given application.

4.1 Risk identification and documentation

Risk events that occur during the execution of a project generally lead to a reduction or loss of profit[14]. With the benefit of hindsight, most risks that arise could have been prevented or the impact of the risk reduced if management action had been taken at an earlier stage in the programme. The risks were present from day one.

Risks do not belong to individuals or departments even though individuals and departments may be responsible for the managing out of the risk. They belong to the company, and it is the company that bears the responsibility for resolving the consequences of the risk should it occur. It is the company and/or the customer who will suffer if any risks are not managed professionally, resulting in financial loss, late deliveries, reduced performance and customer dissatisfaction. It is therefore essential that risks are brought out into the open, where they may be scrutinised by the parties involved, and evaluated to determine their importance, potential consequences and best means to prevent them from turning a project into a disaster. This process includes the identification of the individual or department best suited to manage the risk on behalf of the company.

By making use of foresight to replace hindsight and providing a framework that imposes a rigorous method for identifying risks, *RISKMAN* encourages

---

[14]Risks identified tend to be negative in their impact!

management to take on risks and enables decisions to be made on an informed basis.

Many companies believe that by identifying the risks at an early stage, that they may price themselves out of the market. This may be the case if risks are identified and cost contingencies included, without fully evaluating and changing current bad practices within the estimating and decision-taking activities and without due consideration of the alternative paths open to management to mitigate the effect of risks. It is unfortunate that if the full potential effect of risks are not understood before entering a negotiation that will lead to an increase in the risk exposure. It is a management prerogative to accept the risks.

4.1.1 Methods of identification

The *RISKMAN* methodology enables a company to introduce risk management into their procedures at three levels of complexity, depending upon the management style and capabilities, and on the needs of the market being targeted. Risk identification is a key factor in all three levels of application.

Risk identification is required to be rigorously carried out if the maximum benefit is to be achieved. It is practice in most companies to carry out risk identification, by reliance upon intuitive assessments from the most experienced senior managers. In many cases, when projects have been won and implementation commenced, the contracts have turned into disasters or the profit expectations not realised. Investigations of such projects have shown that the risks were either:

present and known about from day one; or

risks were built-in through the project team being unaware of the factors that gave rise to risks, and the lack of a methodology to adequately identify and communicate risks and manage them when they occur; or

risk identification was not progressed on a tiered basis down to the lowest level of manageable activity.

Risk identification may be approached by a combination of methods:

use of experienced intuitive management;

use of experts in departments;

standard questionnaires and checklists;

use of expert computer-based systems;

structured interviews;

brainstorming sessions;

use of outside specialists/consultants.

Intuitive: Reliance upon intuition on the part of experienced managers, on its own, has proven to be unsatisfactory in the past. Particular difficulties are that managers see risks arising based on their own specialisation and background experiences. These may not, in many instances, be easily related to the project under evaluation.

Managers change and adapt attitudes according to their perception of the risks. They consider that the risks they have identified are their risks, or if identified by others, they are reluctant to accept the risks as theirs to resolve.

When seeking to win projects or release of funds in competition against other equally important activities, managers may understate the risks or even hide them. Therefore, should this method be used, it requires to be supported by some other means to overcome these shortcomings.

Company Experts: Reliance upon company experts, on their own, has proved to be unreliable, generally because they are too involved within the company. Their time may be shared between many projects, or if they are totally committed, they may tend to play down the effect of risks because they are confident of being able to cope with them. However, it may not be them who have to resolve the risk at some later date, and it must be recognised that each person's productivity and capability are different.

There is also a reluctance to openly reveal and discuss risks with others outside of their specialisation. They tend to believe that the risks in their activities belong to them and fail to realise the impact of the risks on others, or to follow the consequences of risks through to their end.

When potential risks are drawn to their attention they feel slighted that they did not see the risk, and may fail to acknowledge that a problem exists.

If the culture of the company is changed to one of openness and risk-taking, and there is a methodology in place to enforce strict risk management, then, as a first port of call, the company experts are the best people to identify risks. They understand the nature of the business, the problems in their field, and the organisation available to manage them out.

Standard Questionnaires and Checklists: As aids to memory, standard questionnaires and checklists are a useful, but not necessarily an effective way of stimulating the identification of risks. On their own, questionnaires are not sufficiently thought-stimulating nor are they effective in dealing with dynamic situations that exist within business and projects.

Key Information

Project _____
WBS Code: _____ Risk No.: ____ Amendment No.: _____ Project Mgr.: _____

Risk Name: _____
Originator: _____ Date Raised/Amended: _____

Summary Information

Level of risk unacceptable ❑   High ❑   Medium ❑   Low ❑   Area of concern ❑
(mark one box)

Probability of Occurrence: _____ %

Risk Cost: £ _____   Calculated Risk Value: £ _____   Adjusted Risk Value: £ _____

Schedule Impact: _____ weeks   Schedule Impact Allowance: _____ weeks

Risk Category: Technical ❑   Resource ❑   Contractual ❑

(mark relevant boxes) Subcontractor ❑   External ❑   Other ❑
                          Other: _____

Detail Information

Description of Risk, Findings & Supporting Evidence:

Is an Avoidance Plan possible? _____   Where documented: _____
Recommended Risk Strategy:
Contingency Plan with Risk Cost calculation

Reasons for adjusting Risk Value:_____

Action Responsibility (name): _____   To be next reviewed by (date): _____

Signatures: Project Manager: _____   Project Director: _____
                          Date: _____   Date: _____

Figure 4.1 Sample risk identification form for intermediate level
***RISKMAN* application**

Checklists may require modifying to suit individual projects and, unfortunately, encourage those persons too lazy or too busy to think about the questions to just tick the box.

Nevertheless, questionnaires are an essential tool in risk management. Whilst they may create or hide problems if they are not properly used or updated, they can also be a most effective method for extracting risks and capturing corporate experience during their preparation and their subsequent use by others. It is recommended that questionnaires should be used in support of one or more of the other identification methods.

A key feature of standard questionnaires is their ability to be integrated directly into the cost identification cycle with the risk forms (sample shown in Figure 4.1) being issued at the same time as the estimate forms.

Standard questionnaires are easily related to the WBS and deliverables and the individuals completing the questionnaires can have time to think about the contents without peer pressures being present. They lend themselves to any formal method of reporting of risks, and can be tailored to obtain standard response formats to ease subsequent evaluation.

Checklists are a simplified form of questionnaire, and can be an effective means of capturing and using corporate knowledge to assist in the process of risk identification. Checklist support should be embedded in any support tool for risk management. However, checklists also have a disadvantage which must be watched carefully. If they are modifiable (which they should easily be, so they can keep up with growth in corporate knowledge), they tend to grow organically, but rarely to contract. This means that using them becomes an increasingly laborious and tedious activity. On completion of running down a lengthy checklist, people heave a sigh of relief and get a cup of coffee. This is a shame because their true value should be in stimulating creative thought and lateral thinking.

Expert Systems: These may be developed using corporate experience assisted by specialists in each discipline involved in the project. They do tend to be expensive to produce and maintain, particularly if the range of projects, customers and technology is extremely wide.

Expert systems rarely reveal risks that are hidden and tend to concentrate people's attention on the obvious. They may work on the basis of asking abstract questions whose relationship to the project are not obvious, and purpose difficult to see. They can create resentment within users who object to reacting with computers. The output may not be presented in a format that supports the management of the risks and may require further interpretation before passing to higher management. There may be difficulties in relating the risk to the WBS and programme, which can make it difficult to manage the financial contingency.

The major benefits of expert systems have been found in areas where the range of risks has been soundly identified over many similar projects, where corporate experience is soundly based in the market, and the company's experts and senior managers have considerable experience to draw on. Should the product, project, business or market change, or even the management team, then the expert system may prove of little use without major modification.

Despite the above problems, expert systems are improving and their development continues. There is still insufficient evidence that expert systems will identify all the major risks and most of the remaining risks within a project, and their use should, therefore, be treated with caution.

Structured Interviewing: Structured interviewing is a technique that has been used successfully for many years both by personnel departments and consultants to extract information. It has also been successfully used by risk/project managers in identifying the potential risks in a project.

The structure of the interview is prepared in advance, making use of pre-prepared discussion material and questionnaires, and arranging the interview to take place in a relaxed atmosphere, away from distractions. Interviews may be on a one-to-one or many-to-one basis.

The prime aim is to get a risk-revealing discussion going that draws out the risks, or, as they may be expressed, concerns, doubts, reservations, qualms, etc., about the activity that has to be undertaken. The questionnaires may be used to stimulate areas of discussion that have not been addressed or as a checklist to confirm that the subject has been researched in depth. This can give the technique some of the advantages of brainstorming whilst limiting the cost, and avoiding its problems.

The many-on-one interview, conducted by several staff from different functional areas with different interests or aims, has the advantage that a wider range of discussion can take place, enabling the subject to be viewed from different perspectives. The problem is that the interviewee may feel threatened or under pressure, and the exercise is clearly costly.

Time is the important element. It is essential that the search for risks is rigorously carried out if the benefits are to be realised later in the programme. However, structured interviewing in the many-to-one situation can be time-consuming, and in addition many concerns and risks will be expressed and all must be recorded, and analysed to determine their importance.

Brainstorming: Brainstorming is an extremely effective method for identifying risks and their mitigation strategies. However, it requires that the major functional and support area specialists and/or managers with a thorough knowledge of the project, be brought together on a number of occasions to discuss in-depth each area and potential solutions.

Brainstorming sessions are subject to being dominated by the stronger personalities, some of whom may wish to push their pet ideas into the project, or use it to enhance their careers. The weaker voices, when trying to express their concerns or specific risks, may feel threatened by the stronger personalities. A skilled and experienced facilitator is essential to encourage and maintain a balance in the discussion.

Brainstorming sessions can also be counter-productive in that they may tie up experienced staff for many hours to the detriment of other programmes.

Outside Specialists/Consultants: This can be an effective means of augmenting existing staff and bringing in additional experience in the fields of concern in the short term.

The major problems with the use of specialists/consultants, are the time it takes for them to become familiar with the project, organisation and procedures of the company, the direct costs involved, and the fact that when they leave, experience leaves with them. However, despite the short-comings, their familiarity with their specialist field should enable them to immediately contribute to the project risk identification and mitigation process, and because of the roving nature of their mission in life, they may be able to bring new and novel solutions to risk mitigation.

Incorporation of risk identification in the estimating process: risk identification should be incorporated into the estimating process. Whether estimating is done centrally or not, estimates should always be signed off by Work Package Managers before incorporation into the budget. This means that individuals responsible for work at the lowest level of a developing Work Breakdown Structure should always be involved in the estimating process, and they should be charged with and trained to identify and document risks in their area before approving any budgetary estimate. This should include risk of saving money and/or time as well as risk of needing to increase budgetary allowance. It should also include safety and reliability risks which may not have financial or schedule impact.

Project:	*Windform Design*		Estimate No.:	*200893*	
WBS Ref.:	*1920*	**Activity:**	*Design main drive struts*		

	Likelihood Estimate			
Risk Appraisal Category	**Nil**	**Low**	**Medium**	**High**
1. **Requirement Specification Status**		*X*		
2. **Our Technical Knowledge**		*X*		
3. **Experience Strength**		*X*		
4. **Resource availability**		*X*		
5. **Response Time To Plan And Estimate**			*X*	
6. **Ability To Meet Project Timescales**		*X*		
7. **Design Standards Availability**				*X*
8. **Reliability/Maintainability/Availability**				*X*
9. **Likelihood Of Acceptance**		*X*		
10. **Status Of Internal Estimates**			*X*	
11. **Status Of External Estimates**				*X*
12. **Subcontractor Availability**		*X*		

13. **Impact %**	*30*		14. **Likelihood %**	*60*
15. **Schedule Impact (Days/Wks/Mths)**	*5 months*		16. **Cost Impact**	*yes*

17 For each category checked 'high', state reason for this selection and mitigation
    action recommended (use space below and supplement sheets as necessary).
    7 material specifications not available.
    *8 reliability specified is very high. The lack of specifications until late in the
        programme willprevent our confirming the figures in time to deliver.*
    11 supplier prices are not fixed until the specification is available.

18. **Uniquely describe the risk for this WBS activity in a few words**

Drive strut material will not meet specification

19. **Trigger event**   :   *WBS item 1821*

Prepared By:	**Dept.:**	**Date:**
Approved By:	**Dept.:**	**Date:**

Figure 4.2 Sample risk identification form

Adopting this approach means that risk is identified at all levels in the Work Breakdown Structure. If a company uses an estimating procedure which gets estimates approved only at low levels, missing out some of the levels in the WBS, then a special procedure must be adopted to incorporate risk identification at those levels. The reason for this is that consequential risks, and accumulated consequential risks may be missed (by *accumulated consequential risks*, we mean that multiple risk occurrences may have a synergistic effect). A special form has been developed to identify consequential risk of this nature (see Figure 4.5).

The greatest danger with risk analysis is that consequential risks and combinations of risks are under-estimated at the early stages of a project life-cycle, when designs are at a concept stage. The *RISKMAN* methodology has gone to some lengths to improve risk identification at the early stages when it is both difficult and crucial because budgeting decisions are being made, by promoting the use of Ishikawa diagrams, described in Section 3.2.6.

4.1.2 Risk identification activity

Every company should seek to adopt a risk identification method that is suited to its culture and organisation, and to meet the depth of detail to which it initially plans its projects.

A company that has in place formal methods for its estimating process may prefer to develop standard risk response forms of the type shown in Figure 4.1.

Companies with a participatory style of management may prefer the brainstorming sessions with the risk or project manager taking the record of the risks. These risks need to be related to the WBS.

A mixture of the standard questionnaires and structured interviewing techniques supported with specialists and/or consultants, does provide a sound basis for in-depth research and identification of risks, but may not be justified on cost grounds.

In the *RISKMAN* methodology, each risk must be uniquely identified by a reference number, and by its description.

The risk must be related to a specific activity[15], though one activity may have any number of risks associated with it.

---

[15]An activity may be defined in different organisations at any level in the WBS.

4.1.3 Standard forms and *RISKMAN*

Comparison between the form shown in Figure 3.35 and 4.1 and 4.2 will show considerable overlaps. They come from different standard form sets. There is no standard form set specifically recommended by *RISKMAN*. However, considerable guidance on forms design, and a wide variety of options will be provided in the *RISKMAN* Implementation Guide Manual.

(OPL) companies have had considerable experience of implementing risk management in organisations throughout the western world, and have found that many of them have considerable difficulty accepting a standard form for internal use. They prefer to modify it.

Flexibility is required in forms design, particularly for a methodology such as *RISKMAN* with its three levels of application (see Section 3.1), especially where these levels represent three ideal types on a spectrum, and where a particular organisation may need, for example, to implement the comprehensive level of risk management whilst having staff who have a relatively low risk maturity level. This means that they may, for example, opt for low/medium/high options on probability without requesting more precise quantification. They may, for example, only require the risk identifier to indicate if there is a direct cost impact and have someone else have the task of quantifying that. They may want the identifier to itemise and quantify a contingency plan and they may not. They may want that contingency plan documented in detail, or they may want to restrict such documentation to two lines of text on the basis that it should be broken out later under what is sometimes called the *rolling wave planning* philosophy. See Figure 4.2 for an example of such a form.

Standard forms design is a very sensitive issue. Some organisations with a decentralised management structure may want to leave a considerable amount of flexibility to the programme manager, project manager, or even work package manager. Others with a centralised power-base and a red-tape culture may object to too much flexibility, particularly if they are hide-bound with, for example, ISO9001 registration which imposes stringent controls on changes to procedures. The *RISKMAN* team have focused on project risk management, and must not be drawn into philosophical discussions about which management style is better or worse. *RISKMAN* must be flexible enough to be adopted as a methodology by any organisation, regardless of its culture. As a result, forms design is part of the tailoring process which must be undergone in applying *RISKMAN*. The *RISKMAN* manuals will provide as much help and guidance as possible to reduce the pain and cost of that process, but it is not possible to avoid it completely if *RISKMAN* is to remain a methodology and avoid being simply a rigid set of procedures.

4.2 Risk quantification

Quantification can be considered as a two stage activity. Stage 1 is the initial estimation of an impact and probability for each risk. Stage 2 is the use of the impact and probability estimates with a model that may be as simple as a spreadsheet to arrive at a quantitative estimate of the effect on timescales and costs.

4.2.1 Impact and probability estimates

Every risk must be assessed for its likelihood of occurrence and estimated impact on timescales, costs and performance (quality).

The person most capable of estimating the risk in an activity is the person who is responsible for that activity or for managing the activity. This person is known as the risk owner. His job with regard to risk quantification is to judge the likelihood of it occurring and its impact should it occur,

The risk owner may, in a subcontract situation be another company or department, however if at all possible the risk should be assigned to a named person within the organisation who fully understands the risk and can evaluate the likely impact and follow-on consequences. The project or risk manager should evaluate the effect of the consequences right through to their end.

Estimates of the likelihood (probability) and impact or risks are based on intuition and experience and may be given in different formats as follows:

- PROBABILITY:

    0-100%

    Low/Medium/High

    Scale value 0-1

- IMPACT:

    Nil/Low/Medium/High

    Cost (in currency units or man days/man months)

    Timescales weeks/months/years

    Quality/performance (reduced specification).

All impacts have an effect on either timescales, cost, performance, or on all three factors. Many impacts have an effect on schedule. In each such case, the risk impact should be quantified in time **as well** as cost and quality. Since an impact on time or quality/performance is generally associated with some form of financial penalty, it follows that all risk impacts can be resolved into a cost contingency. A risk analysis is not complete until all major risks are evaluated in terms of their total cost impact, and due allowance has been made for minor and residual risks. Appendix E provides details of quantification techniques sorted by risk classes.

In the *RISKMAN* Methodology the probabilities when given in high/medium/low format are related to actual figures by converting the scale to numerical quantities using conversion factors. For example:

high to a scale value between 0.3-1.0 (30-100%);

medium to a scale value between 0.1-0.3 (10-30%);

low to a scale value between 0.0-0.1 (0-10%).

Note that any element with a risk likelihood greater than an agreed figure, say 50% should be treated as a programme item not a risk item as it is more likely to occur than not.

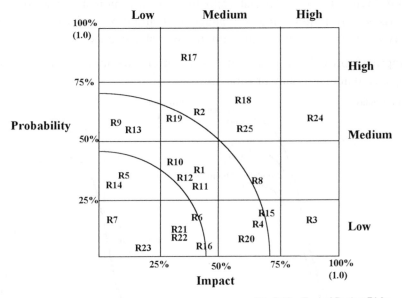

R1 - R25 = Typical Project Risks

Figure 4.3 Project risk probability/impact chart

4.2.2 Final quantification

The project manager or risk manager[16], having received the initial impact and probability estimates now uses these estimates to arrive at values that can be used to evaluate the risks.

---

[16]The job title naturally varies from company to company, industry to industry, and project to project. In very many small projects, the project manager has to perform this task himself, or may have to use the services of a specialist subcontractor.

In one approach, the impact and probabilities may be entered into a spreadsheet or database and converted to a Risk Factor.

The Risk Factor (RF) can be defined mathematically as the interaction between the Probability (P) and Impact (I) when the scale values 0-1 are used:

$$RF=P+I-(P*I)$$

The risk factor can be used as follows:

- Determine which risks are of significant magnitude to warrant a mitigation strategy.

- To factor the risk cost contingency estimate.

- To prioritise risks for reporting and management purposes.

The risks can also be entered onto a risk probability/impact chart to show how the risk exposure is spread within a programme. Analysis of such a chart, as shown in Figure 4.3, with the risks spread as shown, indicates that only a few of the risks may require higher management attention and that the greater majority of the risks are in the medium to low risk category.

This approach provides a picture of risk sensitivity without having to quantify the impacts in actual money or time limits.

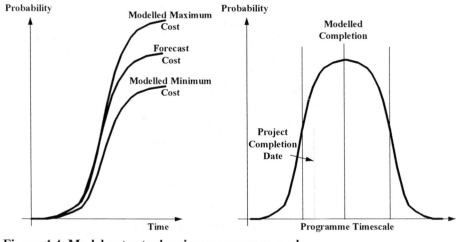

Figure 4.4 Model outputs showing exposure spread

If the *RISKMAN* methodology is applied at the comprehensive level, then all risks that can affect timescales or costs are entered into a project risk model to enable the total risk exposure within the programme timescales and costs to be assessed and quantified.

The basis for quantification is assessment of data that is itself derived from best guess, intuition or previous experience. The results of modelling the data to quantify the spread of exposure, are themselves subject to question. Modelling and quantifying the data does, however, enable the results to be more closely related to the variations in the likely out-turn of the project in costs and timescales.

Figure 4.4 shows typical model outputs. The important point to note is that a spread of exposure is shown. This spread enables management to base their current decisions and future plans on the likely out-turn of the project, rather than on a traditional deterministic forecast that has generally proven to be optimistic in the first place.

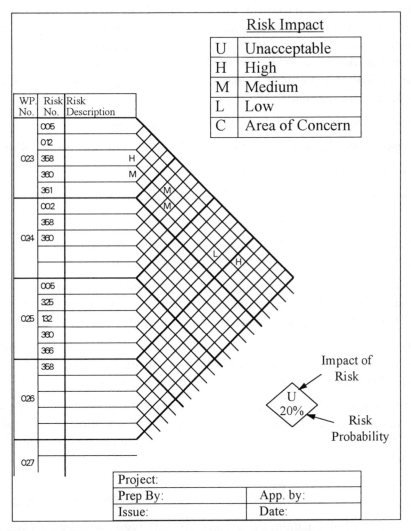

Figure 4.5 Example form for recording risk interactions

When estimating the affect of risks on a programme it must be borne in mind that risks may interact with each other and that for some activities there may be more than one risk to its success.

Risks may not interact with another risk until much later in the programme though the likelihood that they will interact may be known earlier if the consequences are assessed. Figure 4.5 shows a form that may be used to identify those risks that may interact with one and other.

4.3 Risk prioritising and filtering

To assist the risk management process, *RISKMAN* requires that risks are graded and sorted to aid management in recognising and controlling the major (important) ones. We have identified a number of methods for classifying and categorising risk in the *RISKMAN* methodology, as described up to this point. These methods are provided to assist in the task of prioritising and filtering the risks and are summarised below:

In Chapter 2 we introduced the *RISKMAN* 12 classes of risk.

In Chapter 2 we also introduced the *RISKMAN* categories of risk as follows:

- Category 1 - cost effect only,
- Category 2 - contingency plans and costs affected,
- Category 3 - programme contingency and cost affected.

We have also introduced the concept of calculating risk exposure and/or risk factor that measures the weighting that may be given to a risk.

Every risk that is identified belongs within a particular class, and as previously explained, this enables us to more easily identify a risk owner to manage the risk. It also enables risks to be prioritised for management purposes.

On a major project in some of the risk classes, e.g. technical, there may be many hundreds of risks identified, and these in turn may be listed in sub-classes of risk associated with particular project activities.

One of the first tasks that must be undertaken is the prioritising of the risks such that only the high priority ones are given full attention at this point in time. The risk weighting indicated by exposure value or factor enables this to be done easily and quickly.

Under each class of risk we can now reduce the risks down to those that are worthy of management's immediate attention, e.g. top 30 risks in each class.

However, in a bid situation, the project manager requires to be able to select those risks that will have major impact in the cost area as early as possible and to seek mitigation strategies to reduce the costs to acceptable levels. This can be done by filtering the risks using the three categories identified above.

By categorising the risks we can also identify those risks in each class that may have a major effect on the programme timescales.

Risks we have also identified in Chapter 3 have an active time period from when they are created through until the consequences are finally resolved. During this active life, we also identified a generation time period when the risk is actually generated by the events that trigger the start of the risk.

This provides another means of filtering risks for reporting purposes. By trigger date. The earlier in the programme that the risk is triggered into being, the more important it is that a mitigation strategy is in place ready to be implemented.

For the purposes of management, the risks can now be prioritised and filtered into importance by their classification, weighting, risk category and by their imminence in time.

4.4 Processing and presentation of risk data

In paragraph 4.2 above we mentioned the use of models to support risk management. It is not, however, necessary to use sophisticated models, a simple spreadsheet will often suffice.

The necessary action is to process the data to achieve the needs of the project and the company. Risk management is not a single activity that can be dropped between in-house and external projects. It must become a part of the company culture, used at all times to support the decision-making process with strict records maintained of the reasoning behind specific decisions forming a part of the history of the business. When things do go wrong the facts will then be available to determine why they went wrong: the lessons will be of value to the current project and will certainly benefit future projects.

The *RISKMAN* methodology calls for a simple database of the risks in a project to be constructed from day one and this should contain, at a minimum, the following risk data:

- Risk description;
- Risk identity number;
- Activity at risk/work breakdown reference;
- Risk owner reference/work package manager;
- Risk cause ownership references;

- Risk impact estimate;
- Risk probability estimate;
- Risk exposure as calculated;
- Risk exposure as adjusted (where applicable);
- Risk trigger indicator;
- Risk mitigation strategy.

Assuming the risk database has a spreadsheet capability and access to a forms processing system, then the database could be expanded to include or provide the following:

- Risk priority listing;
- Risk register: detailed list of all risks, or all major risks, recorded in the database in order of importance;
- Risk summary: single line listing of risks;
- Risk owner's bid summaries: lists of risks and causes by ownership;
- Risk trigger status: list of risks by trigger event date;
- Project manager's monthly risk status report;
- Risk statistics: Clear up rate, risks outstanding, new risks identified.

Date	Risk No.	Description	Risk Budget		Risk Value	Project risk status
			Value added /subtracted	Total remaining	Current Risk Value	Risk Cost
Project Start	All Risks					

Figure 4.6 Example Risk Log

It is essential that the project manager reports on the financial status of the contingency at the same time as the project financial status is reported. The monitoring and reporting of risk contingency spend, together with project liabilities and cash flow status, when compared with the previous month's values and the estimates available at commencement of the project, provides higher management with an easily assessable picture of the status of the project and hence the project's risk management.

Figure 4.6 shows a typical Risk log that may be used for monitoring and reporting on contingency spend, and which should have an entry each time there is a risk occurrence or a change to the status of any project risk. This includes recording when risks have gone away.

The build-up of the costs in a project was depicted in Figure 3.24; this type of illustration may be adapted to present the costs to higher management when reporting on the consumption of contingency funds.

4.5 Risk mitigation strategies

4.5.1 Introduction

Risk mitigation is the action required to reduce, eliminate or avert the potential impact of risks on a project. In many cases it is presented as a future plan of action or strategy. Risk mitigation planning requires to be implemented at each stage in a project's life cycle, following completion of the risk assessment and quantification process.

A mitigation strategy is normally identified for risks with a high or medium likelihood and impact assessment or those classed as unacceptable risks or critical risks.

For each risk that is so identified the project management team must evaluate the alternative paths open to mitigate the risk and select the most appropriate plan.

In doing this work it is essential that the mitigation path is evaluated for its consequences right through to the end of the programme.

Residual risks will normally be considered as subject to mitigation either by an increase in the residual risk contingency fund or by the company accepting that the risk exposure created by these risks is manageable, within current procedures and therefore the risks are acceptable.

4.5.2 Mitigation paths

The paths open to project managers to mitigate risk are shown in process format in Figure 4.7 and described in the paragraphs that follow.

Avoidance: This path is mainly directed at removing the cause of the risk by analysing the situation to determine the elements that are creating the risk. When this cannot be achieved, the avoidance path has to be approached with care as it can involve making decisions such as writing off previous investment, or putting the investment at risk through not achieving the business aims. This path includes:

Deciding not to continue with a product or to no-bid a project in which the risk exposure to the company is perceived to be too high.

Leaving the risk with the customer where the customer is believed to be in the best position to mitigate the risk, or that a more acceptable price may be achieved. This path may not be acceptable to the customer.

The acceptance of an alternative lower risk technology path, which may lead to reduced quality performance, or to a less acceptable solution.

Insisting that escape clauses are included in the contract which release the supplier if the risk occurrence happens.

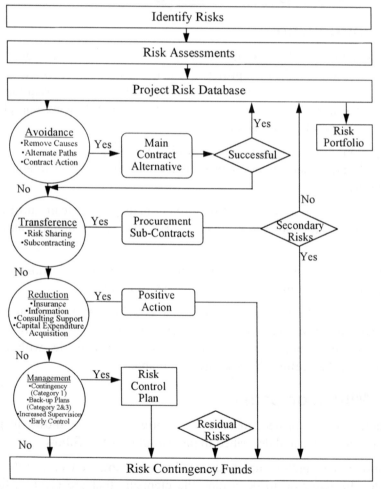

Figure 4.7 Risk Mitigation Paths

Transference: This comprises passing the risks onto others more capable of managing their risks. Generally, this means transferring the activity onto subcontractors who understand the subject and are more capable of identifying and mitigating the risks involved. However this is also a path that has to be approached with care.

> Subcontractors increase their costs to cover any increase in their risks. The liability of subcontractors will be less than that of the prime contractors and should the risks be incurred then only the costs that lie within the liability of the subcontractors contract will be recoverable.

> Within this path lies the ability to enter into joint ventures or risk-sharing agreements to reduce the level of risk on each member to an acceptable position. Each of these relationship paths must be assessed for risks hidden within the undertaking of its management.

Reduction: The reduction risk path generally requires some up-front investment such as taking out an insurance policy, purchase of capital equipment items or forward buying of foreign currency.

> The purpose of the reduction path is to take an action, generally a single action that will reduce the risk to an acceptable level. Since this path mainly relies upon expenditure of money, it invariably increases costs, e.g. the amount of insurance premium.

> Within the reduction path also lies the ability to procure information or the services of specialist consultants to support the project team in their activities. The company may also need to make a capital investment to meet the programme requirements, either in equipment or by prototyping.

> This path also addresses those risks that involve a choice of technology or programme activity where an extra cost may be involved, but the impact of the risk reduction will not affect other factors within the programme such as timescales or performance.

Management: This path comprises the majority of the risk that gives rise to daily problems for the project manager.

> In general this path contains those risks that require continuous management activity until the risks are managed out. The activities include regular monitoring of progress, continuous assessment of resources assigned to alleviating the risk, increases in expenditure or tighter control of finances. It is therefore possible for project managers to pull in margins at critical points in order to create reserves for resolving other risks as they arise.

> The major risks that fall into this category will require trigger events to be inserted or identified within the project network.

The capability of the project manager to exercise control earlier in the programme to prevent risks occurring, and to impose tighter reporting and monitoring procedures is important for this category.

Included in this path is the pre-preparation of fall-back (back-up) plans that can be put in place ready for use should it become evident that a risk will occur.

Contingency: The contingency path provides funds to cover those risks that are assessed to be of a low likelihood and impact, and for risks that have not been revealed during the identification process, i.e. the residual risks. Under this path is also that category of risks that exist within any concerns, doubts or apprehensions that are expressed. Concerns may turn into risks further into a project, if they are neglected. These types of risks show themselves during the implementation of the activity.

The more thoroughly risk management is implemented, the lower the number of residual risks that require to be catered for within this category and the higher the likelihood that they will fall into a lower impact rating.

Residual risks and concerns may be mitigated either by inclusion of a sum of money within the risk contingency or, subject to senior management's confidence in their risk management methodology, the acceptance of the risk exposure.

All of the above mitigation paths require an investment trade-off to be considered between the funding to be included for risk contingency for the path selected and the cost or savings to be made if an alternative path is taken.

Pre-Bid Stage	**Bid Stage**	**Implementation**
		Contract Acceptance
	ITT Evaluation	Project Start-up
	Subcontractor Selection	Detailed Design
	Team Member Selection	Development
Marketing	Initial Sytem Design	Production
Business Plan	Risk Assessment	Integration
Product Plans	Project Planning	Testing
Project Plans	Bid Proposal Production	Installation
Project Tracking	Technical Trade-Offs	Commissioning
Supplier Identification	Logistic Support Requirements	Acceptance
Subcontract Identification	PBS / WBS / OBS Development	Operation
Competitor Analysis	Cash Flow Development	Warranty
Customer Relations	Investment Requirements	Maintenance
Investment Profiles	Risk Contingency Estimating	Support
	Cost Estimating	Disposal
	Risk Exposure / Price Approvals	
	Management Plans Development	

Figure 4.8 Project Stages

4.5.3 Relating mitigation strategy to project stage

Risk management activities can be described within the following stages in a project:

- Pre-bid stage: this is the initial investment stage and includes the market research, prospective project tracking and speculative product/technology research and development. It also includes the period when prime contractors form initial working agreements with potential subcontractors and suppliers (see Figure 4.8.

- Bid stage: this stage, particularly for a prime contractor, may require considerable investment. The stage includes the work involved in preparation of the proposal and the contract negotiation (see Figure 4.8.)

  Equipment manufacturers may find that their product maturity must be increased, or new features added before the bid can be submitted. Preliminary designs must be evaluated and trade-offs completed.

  Initial agreements between prime contractors, suppliers and subcontractors must be finalised. Where essential to increase chances of winning and reduce risks, teaming, consortiums or joint venture arrangements put in place.

  It is during this stage that risk analysis imposes the greatest workload on the project manager (and/or risk manager). Risks to successful achievement of the programme must be identified, assessed, and mitigation methods planned and in some programmes implemented. As part of the price build-up, the mitigation process risk contingencies must be estimated, and approval decisions obtained from senior management.

- Implementation stage: this covers the work involved in design, development, production, testing, integration, installation, commissioning , acceptance, warranty and support. This is the stage where the benefits of using effective risk management show, through improved project risk handling, performance, increased profits or for existing programmes in reducing unplanned expenditure(see Figure 4.8).

The objective with mitigation strategies is to effectively replace hindsight with improved foresight. However, where risks do arise during a programme it is necessary to have an approved methodology in place for their management and control.

Appendix F provides a table of typical risk mitigation techniques related to the twelve *RISKMAN* risk classes.

4.5.4 Pre-bid mitigation activities

During the pre-bid stage strategic and commercial risks to success must be rigorously searched out and mitigation plans be put in place and implemented for the unacceptable and critical risks that are identified. The aim is to protect the company's investment and to prevent wasted investment of both money and resources.

RISKMAN identifies the following twelve classes of risk:

strategic	master plan	organisational
marketing	definition	operational
contractual	process	maintenance
financial	product	external

During the pre-bid stage the following classes of risk are of major importance:

- Strategic - company objectives, image and importance of project.

- Marketing - market position, competitor analysis, customer relations/project tracking and selling strategy.

- Contractual - supplier/subcontractor/teaming, commercial arrange-ments and information protection.

- Master plan - customer/product timescales.

- External - socio-political and environmental issues as well as health and safety issues.

This does not mean that the risks in the other classes are ignored, only that at this stage their importance in the decision process and their effect on the investment cost is generally less than those given above.

At the pre-bid stage strategic risks are very important. The risk identification process will have revealed the risk elements. These risks must be resolved otherwise commitment by the company will be less than wholehearted and may not be forthcoming when the need arises.

Management are generally reluctant to commit resources to resolve problems and support market activities where it is perceived that the company itself is not committed.

A major part of the mitigation of strategic risks is therefore orientated to achievement of commitment. The project or product must align with the strategic aims and business intentions of the company. Failure in this area will normally result in the project or product being stopped.

Risks to market position are generally subject to mitigation either by improved products, promotions, increased sales activities, competitor buy-outs, amalgamation or price reductions. All of these areas generally require increased investment effectively increasing the risk budget. Any such increases will normally only be given if commitment to the companies' presence in the market has been obtained.

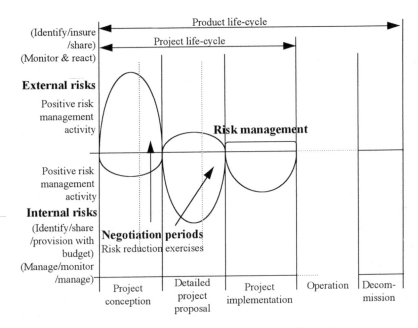

Figure 4.9 Emphasis of risk activity throughout life-cycle

It may also be feasible to transfer some of the strategic risk by entering a partnership or a joint venture arrangement.

Achievement of business objectives, product development, and bidding to win projects require considerable investment on the part of a company. There are many ways of financing such activities and the risks that require mitigation will depend upon how the financing was organised at the start.

External risks are particularly important because they are not truly controllable or manageable. As we have indicated earlier in Section 2.1.3, all risks accepted when a go-ahead is given - have to be *managed*.

External risks need particularly careful consideration at this early stage, particularly at times of major political upheaval - such as the ending of the cold war.

4.5.5 Bid stage mitigation activities

It is during the bid stage (see Figure 4.8) that the *RISKMAN* methodology is likely to have its most significant impact. Risks have to be rigorously searched out, not only within the Invitation to Tender (ITT) or Request for Quotation (RFQ) documentation, but also within each deliverable and work activity.

For effective management and mitigation, risks should be related to the Work Breakdown Structure (WBS), to the Product Breakdown Structure (PBS), and to the Organisation Breakdown Structure (OBS). In the matrix[17] management environment found in most large and mature project-based organisations, the OBS is embedded in the Cost Breakdown Structure (CBS). Provided that the accounting systems are set up correctly, this can enable responsibility for risks and causes, as well as ownership of work packages themselves to be linked into the organisation's main-frame systems. This in turn can be extremely helpful in monitoring and control of both the project's main plan, and its risks and contingency plan, and this can be easily linked to its financial controls.

The breakdown structures must also relate to the project network for control of the project. The network should be quantitatively analysed to determine the exposure in delivery and, milestone timescales if a networking philosophy is employed. This is most commonly achieved using a master plan network, or at the most with an intermediate level network containing a limited number of high-level activities. Monte Carlo simulation of such a network is a particularly useful tool at this level. If a full cascade philosophy is implemented in the project planning, taking the breakdown to the lowest level of work packages and maybe further to detailed activities at a lower level still, then it is necessary to use a Cost-Time and Resource (CTR) type system such as is common on major oil industry developments. The CTR approach ensures that sub-networks are limited to a manageable size, and are linked using interface milestones. Our comments here do not indicate that a networking approach is essential, even for a comprehensive level application of *RISKMAN*. Risk Analysis applied in this exhaustive way can be very expensive, and can have questionable results in any case. Crude modelling using Gantt techniques can also permit a comprehensive level *RISKMAN* approach to yield effective risk reporting.

A similar analysis should be conducted for the costs. Again, Monte Carlo simulation can be extremely useful here. Monte Carlo simulation software is available for use on costed networks or in spreadsheets. The technique is described briefly in Appendix C. There are numerous variations of the

---

[17]See Effective project management in a matrix management environment by Ned Robins, published in the International Journal of Project Managers, Vol. II, No. 1, February, 1993.

technique using probability distribution curves, approximations such as Controlled Interval and Memory, Latin Hypercube or straightforward three-point analysis. Again, however, most organisations would be making a massive step forward if they use a crude manual analysis with three-point estimates. For example, we can acquire a very good picture of the likely distribution curve for expenditure or schedule by adding optimistic values to arrive at an indication of the lowest number, the pessimistic values for the highest, and similarly for the mean, taking care to make a manual adjustment for the interference factor between the consequential variables. It is then possible to use experience and/or intuition to establish the likely curve (see Figure 4.10).

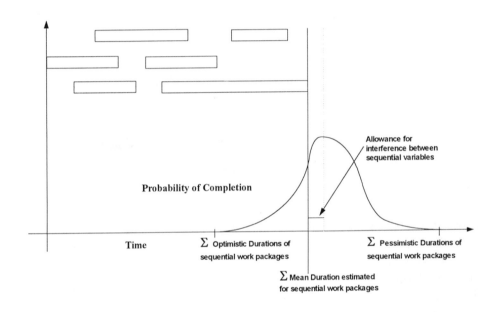

Figure 4.10 Manually-derived probability of achieving schedule

This manual technique can be readily extended with only little additional effort to application combining cost forecasting using three-point analysis. Against each of the work packages, spending is anticipated to arrive at a probabilistic approximation of cash-flow throughout the duration of the project. This can even incorporate an approximation of when the risk contingency fund will be required (see Figure 4.11).

Such an application of *RISKMAN* principles will permit a level of risk modelling which would be regarded as advanced and at a comprehensive level amongst many of the most progressive managements of successful western companies. However, it will require little or no computerised support to implement. Computer systems are invaluable for configuration management and project control, especially when networked. However, the data that we currently have for risk modelling is so crude that they are of hardly any use in the modelling arena at present. This is why the *RISKMAN* team recommend a parametric estimating approach to computerised risk modelling in most industries at present. Only when networked computer systems have been in use for some time, and extensive data-banks of historical project information have been built up, will this situation change drastically.

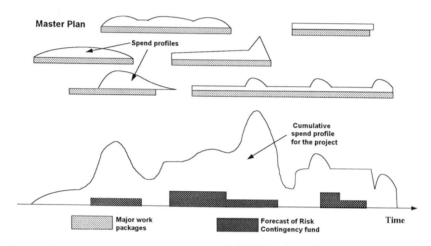

Figure 4.11 Manually-derived estimate of project cash-flow

Risk cost contingency budgets must be estimated and these must be identifiable to the item at risk to provide the strict management of risk budgets that is essential if the benefits of the *RISKMAN* Methodology are to be obtained during the implementation stage. This may mean estimating the risk down to the lowest level of the WBS. However, it must be remembered that, for each item, only the risk exposure is added to the fund. If project sensitivity risk is normal and does not subsequently alter the risk cost, it may represent a small proportion of the actual funding required when a risk occurrence happens (10% for example if the probability is judged to be 0.1). This means that the actual consumption of the risk budget may be very *lumpy* in profile. Senior management need to understand this.

Mitigation strategies must be stringently assessed for their potential effectiveness and for the risks that may exist within them to their successful implementation.

Risks that are identified are formed into a database or risk register, where they can be managed more easily. Within the database the twelve classes of risk that *RISKMAN* provides may be used to categorise the risks and related mitigation strategies.

Mitigation management during the bid activity is primarily concerned with forward planning. The risk mitigation strategies will, in many cases, only be implemented if the bid is won, although some of the strategies may need to be implemented (or conditionally put in place - as in collaborative team-building) during the preparation of the bid response or during contract negotiations, as part of the risk reduction strategy used to implement the win strategy.

Receipt of the RFQ or sufficient details of a customer's requirements, initiates the bid stage risk management activities. *RISKMAN* requires the customer's documentation to be rigorously read by representatives of the functional work areas that will be involved in the bid process (e.g. Commercial, Contracts, Estimating, Technical, Production, Project Management, Customer Support) to search out and identify risks and in particular any major changes to the company's perception of the risks that may adversely increase the risk exposure, and that this must be done promptly so that a decision can be taken on whether or not to proceed with the bid activities. This is therefore the commencement of the strategic risk mitigation activity.

When all risks have been assessed and those risks that require mitigation strategies have been identified under their appropriate classification in the risk database the mitigation strategies can be identified. The 'owner' of the risk is generally the best person to identify the alternative paths and potential problems that may arise if they are taken.

Risk management within the *RISKMAN* Methodology, is concerned with getting risks out into the open where all functional areas, that may be affected by the risk, can assist in developing a clear perception of the risk and the potential paths for mitigation. This must be borne in mind, as a 'brainstorming' session with the relevant parties may reveal a different perception of the validity of the risk, and alternative paths for its mitigation, from those obtained from the risk owners, through checklists or even in one-to-one interviews.

Figure 4.7 shows how each risk must be considered to determine the mitigation path that is more likely to lead to success, though in many cases the actual path is generally obvious to the risk owner.

The greater majority of the mitigation strategies involve the need for extra costs to be allowed for within the risk contingency budget. Whilst these will have been included within the price build-up, against each activity affected, it is unlikely that the initial price estimate will be acceptable to the market if a comprehensive analysis is attempted. Senior management within the company must approve and accept the risk exposure. They may, of course, increase the risks either by taking out money from the risk contingency fund or by reducing the profit level. In some cases arbitrary decisions may be taken to reduce the estimated cost of activities or expense estimates. This is a dangerous habit of senior management, but one which will be both less dangerous, and less readily adopted after the culture change described in Section 2.2. Assumptions may be made about sources and availability of funding of capital items, and again the comments about culture change apply. After the culture change, at least assumptions made in support of decision will be documented and understood at a level down in the organisation where the people who are likely to be tasked with achieving targets within the resulting budget at some point in the future, reside.

RISKMAN requires that such decisions and the factors leading to them, are recorded and that any risk that is increased or new risk created has its mitigation strategy re-assessed or a mitigation plan identified.

Where a project risk model is available it will reveal the spread of exposure within each deliverable, between milestones and within each responsibility area. The model can be used to identify the potential effectiveness of the proposed mitigation strategies.

During contract negotiation mitigation is a key activity. Risks that have to be avoided within the contract must be identified and action taken to include the appropriate clauses. Changes in wording within the technical documentation and bid proposal, as clarification of the project is sought by the customer, may invalidate previously prepared mitigation strategies or require additional strategies to be put in place as new risks are accepted. Care must be taken to avoid taking on new risks inadvertently under the commercial pressures to win the contract.

RISKMAN identifies the major role that subcontractors play in mitigation of the prime contractors risk exposure. During the contract negotiation the prime contractor must ensure that potential changes in risk level and in mitigation strategies, many of which may lie within the subcontractor's responsibility, are fed down to the owners for agreement.

For all the above reasons, *RISKMAN* recommends that the project manager designate is part of, or better still the leader of, the proposal team. If this is not possible, an experienced project manager should be appointed to play this role in his place, and a formal hand-over (transfer) to the actual project manager should take place at contract award.

4.5.6 Implementation stage mitigation activities

Risk mitigation in the implementation stage commences with receipt of the contract or a letter of intent.

RISKMAN requires that, following award of the contract, start-up commences in accordance with defined procedures. The procedures are to effectively reduce start-up risks to a minimum.

According to the *RISKMAN* Methodology the procedures should address the following:

Review of contract upon receipt.

Formal procedure to determine acceptability of the terms offered.

Handover procedure from bid/negotiating team to the project implementation team.

Procedure for up-dating the WBS/OBS matrix and making the resources available in line with the schedule required.

Procedure for risk management during the project implementation, including how new project risks are identified and handled, and also how subcontractors will manage risks.

Procedure for producing an up-dated financial statement for the project to reflect any changes in the costs and contingencies arising from contract negotiations. This should provide the basis for the project manager to monitor and control the project finances including risk contingencies and liabilities.

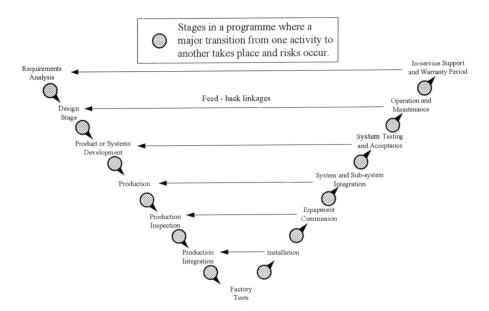

Figure 4.12 Classic 'V' diagram of risk-prone transitions in a project

Most experienced project managers will agree that the majority of project problems are buried in the contractual arrangements made at the time of contract award when, historically, the project manager is recruited.

The risk database should contain all the previously identified risks and their mitigation strategies.   During the implementation the effectiveness of the mitigation strategies defined during the bid stage will be revealed.

Not all projects have a fully defined risk database at contract commencement. The completeness of the database will be dependant upon the resources and time available to complete the bid process. Many of the risks in the database may have been identified as risk areas with the actual risks within the areas undefined at that stage. Under this circumstance the project team will have estimated global contingencies or outlined broad strategies for mitigating the potential risks.

As the project approaches or moves through each of the production and implementation transition stages (see Figure 4.12), the actual risks will be identified and fresh new risks arise (residual risks).

The twelve classes of risk that *RISKMAN* uses are still valid. Any new risks that arise will be entered in the risk database under the appropriate risk class.

The mitigation categories are also still valid. However, avoidance in respect of leaving the risks with the customer is no longer a valid proposition unless a contract variation order is put in place.

The transfer of new and additional risks to subcontractors is also only valid if they accompany a change request, as the subcontractor will also require a contract variation order.

Risks that are to be insured should be held until it is absolutely essential to incur the cost and the full extent of the risk is clearly understood, unless there is danger of the cost of such insurance escalating beyond the risk contingency included in the price.

Risks that require capital to be invested by the company should be thoroughly re-investigated to confirm the requirement and that the appropriate company procedures are implemented to obtain the necessary authorisations.

The project manager has control of the risk contingency budgets. To obtain the benefits (see Chapter 7), he must strictly manage the budgets and project liabilities. Changes in spend without reduction in risk must be investigated. Increases in liabilities without an attendant improvement in the project's status must also be investigated as these indicate a lack of good mitigation management of risks in the internal or the subcontractor's activities.

Any global risk contingencies must be held separate from defined risk contingency budgets. The spend of global budgets would often require additional authorisation other than that of the project manager, particularly if the current total risk exposure remains close to the total risk contingency fund.

The risk owners must continually keep abreast of development in their risk areas. However, the project manager has an overseeing role. He must monitor the risks within the database at regular intervals and check the effectiveness of the mitigation strategies as they are implemented. He must pay particular attention to risks approaching trigger points.

As implementation proceeds into operation and maintenance, the structure of risks changes as well as the owners responsible for their mitigation. For example, the customer may operate the equipment and have the maintenance subcontracted to a third party.

An essential part of risk mitigation is the regular reporting of risk status. On some contracts this may also include reporting of the risk status to the customer or progressing with the customer those risks that he owns.

Risk ID no.	Risk description	Item/activity at risk		Risk owner	Risk factor	Risk mitigation			Remarks
		Description	WBS ref.			Strategy description	Event WBS ref.	Date	
							Trigger		
001									
002									
003									
004									
005									
Issued by Contact Tel. Int. Ext.		PROJECT : SAMPLE RISKMAN RISK REGISTER				Issue number Issue date Update date			

Figure 4.13 Typical risk register format

4.6 Risk monitoring, reporting and control

The *RISKMAN* methodology requires the risks within the risk database, be re-assessed continuously throughout the implementation programme until the risk is managed out.

Risks within the database will normally be printed out in the form of a Risk Register for the purpose of monitoring, control and reporting of the risks. Figure 4.13 shows the format for a typical Risk Register. Production of the risk register should normally be carried out by the risk manager on behalf of the project manager, or on a small project by the project manager.

Risks previously identified and assessed during the bid stage will change as the project matures and transits from one stage to another during the implementation. The changes may be small if the risk management during the bid stage, was very detailed. However, in many cases, the information will not have been available, thus the bid stage risk assessments will have been less rigorous.

It must be noted by management that each risk and its mitigation strategy should have time allocated to their management. Re-assessment of previously identified risks should be undertaken prior to commencement of the stage in the programme at which the risk or in the case of a major risk the trigger event resides.

This will normally allow sufficient time to enable the results of the risk assessment to be judged, strategies for mitigation reviewed, and revised mitigation strategies to be put in place. An aim of this exercise is to prevent the risk impact from escalating beyond the previous estimated value, thus ensuring that the risk contingency is still valid. A secondary aim is to improve the benefit to the company by ensuring that risks are managed out such that the minimum of contingency funds are spent.

New risks as they arise must be just as stringently identified and assessed to ensure that they do not absorb an in-appropriate share of the contingency budget that has been put in place to control such residual risks.

Each new risk must be entered into the risk database and subjected to the same management and reporting as previously identified risks.

A project risk model, if available, should be continuously used by the project team. The model should be used to test the effectiveness of changes proposed to mitigation strategies and/or the effect of strategies proposed to resolve new risks.

Risk Item Description	
	_____
	_____
Item/Activity At Risk and **WBS Reference**	_____
	_____ WBS Ref._____
Estimated Impact **Tick Impact Areas**	Cost Time Performance
Estimate Likelihood of **Occurrence**	High Medium Low
Mitigation Plan Proposed **(If not Risk Owner leave blank)**	_____
	_____
	_____
Proposed Risk Owner	Name: Company: Department: Telephone:
Report Raised By:	_____ Name
	_____ Department
_____ Date	_____ Telephone
Send Copies To:	Risk Manager Project Manager Proposed Risk Owner Financial Manager

Figure 4.14 Typical new risk reporting form

Project risk status and any significant changes to risk's status must be reported at the project manager's regular progress meetings. *RISKMAN* requires that the reports of such meetings should contain a means for identifying the risks that are addressed and for high-lighting any new risks that arise.

In general, the participants at such meetings will mostly be functional managers and specialists who are also risk owners. The reporting of the status of risks is therefore only an extension of the normal reporting function and not an additional task.

The most important issue is the current total project risk exposure when compared to the total remaining risk contingency fund (see risk log, Figure 4.6). It is a good practice to operate a red/amber/green system for the project portfolio managed using the *RISKMAN* method where:

> RED = projects where risk exposure > remaining risk budget, and are automatically reviewed by senior management;

> AMBER = projects where risk exposure > 90% of remaining risk budget and are automatically reported to senior management;

> GREEN = project where risk exposure < 90% of remaining risk budget and are therefore felt to be satisfactorily under control.

(The actual percentages shown above are not prescribed by *RISKMAN*, and different organisations are likely to vary the criteria for their red, amber and green categories of project).

RISKMAN requires that new risks as they arise are drawn to the attention of the project manager and that it is assessed and mitigated in accordance with the now company standard methodology. The reporting function should also preferably record the risk and its characteristics, so that the project manager can commence a risk evaluation as speedily as possible and draw the risk to the attention of others who may be affected.

Figure 4.14 shows a typical *RISKMAN* form that may be used for the new risk reporting activity. Provision is made for the risk to be raised by any member of the team. The project manager or risk manager must then progress the new risk to determine its characteristics.

When reporting the risk status to higher management it is not appropriate to use an up-dated risk register, which may contain a large number of risks. Only those risks that have a significantly high risk factor, or that are likely to overspend their contingency budget, or that have a major impact on performance, cost and timescales need reporting. On a major project such a list is likely to be less than 50 items, and on a small project less than 20 items. Reporting to higher management should reflect the importance of the risks and is therefore carried out using a single line risk summary report typically as shown in Figure 4.15.

RISK SUMMARY							
Risk ID No.	**Brief risk description**	**Brief activity at risk description**	**WBS ref.**	**Risk owner**	**Risk factor mitigation strategy**	**Critical review date**	**Remarks**
0001							
0002							
0003							
0004							
0005							

Figure 4.15 Typical single line risk summary

RISKMAN requires that the risk manager or project manager has automatic access to copies of all minutes of meetings at which risks are likely to be discussed and reported upon.

The project manager reports on risk status to higher management in at least two forms:

- within the regular project status reports, normally with a single-line risk summary report attached, and any major changes to risk status described in the report

- within the project financial status report in the form of changes to the contingency and liabilities.

Unplanned increases in spend of contingencies or major increases in liabilities to subcontractors may indicate that the project is increasingly encountering new risks, that the strategies and contingencies put in place at the start are not working, or that the project is not being well managed. Should any of these factors be apparent then higher management should initiate a project audit.

The *RISKMAN* Methodology recommends regular reviews of the project risk database, preferably chaired by an independent authority from higher management. Reviews would typically concentrate on the major and more imminent risks as well as the new risks, and will mainly be concerned with the effectiveness of the risk mitigation strategies. Such reviews should normally be conducted at quarterly intervals, or more frequently depending on the size and nature of the project.

Representatives on the risk review team will usually include the project and risk managers, the major risk owners and may also include representatives of the customer, if appropriate, particularly if he is a risk owner. The project manager is in control of the project and should not be constrained to adopting any changes in mitigation strategies proposed by such review teams.

Where the project manager disagrees on proposed changes in strategy then it is necessary for the risk to be re-assessed and for all alternative mitigation paths to be reconsidered, before the project manager informs the chairman of the review team of his commitment or otherwise to the strategy proposed. It is the responsibility of the project manager to complete the programme to time, cost and performance constraints.

4.7 Risk audits

The *RISKMAN* Methodology provides for projects to be audited at regular intervals and at other times should any acceptable reasons occur for an audit.

The objectives of the project risk audit are:

- to confirm that risk management in accordance with the company's procedures has been applied at each stage in the project life-cycle;

- to confirm that the project is well managed and that the risks are under control;

- to verify that the project reporting and project management is effective;

- to assist in the transfer across projects of experience gained in resolving risks;

- to assist in identifying early signs of deterioration in the profit potential of the project;

- to verify that the project history file is maintained.

Risk audits do not seek to duplicate any of the quality audit procedures. They are concerned only with the effectiveness of risk management and in particular with increasing management confidence that they will achieve the targets set for the project.

Because of the need to determine the effectiveness of the risk management on the project, the audit is primarily targeted at reconciling the current financial status of the project and the forecast completion status, with the previously reported status and the contract start-up status.

Whilst a project may appear to be out of control it may very well be the case that the project manager is fighting to overcome major undocumented risks that were imposed by earlier higher management, financial or organisational decisions.

4.8 Project completion

Project completion from the *RISKMAN* project risk management view takes place when the work on the contract has been completed, and the project manager can review the effectiveness of the project risk management process.

Using the project history file and the risk database, the project manager is required to analyse the project from start to end, seeking out the unforeseen occurrences and comparing the circumstances with those existing at the start. This project close-down report should spell out conclusions and make recommendations concerning the adequacy of the following as a minimum:

- quality and completeness of the proposal and specifications;
- the initial risk appraisal;
- the contingency funds established at start-up;
- the resources available at each stage of the project;
- subcontractor selection performance and risk management capability;
- the organisation's ability to manage the project;
- soundness of the engineering design and implementation;
- effectiveness of controls of cost, time and quality;
- effectiveness of risk analysis and risk management during the project execution;
- effectiveness of mitigation strategies employed;
- source and nature of unforeseen risks and what needs to be done to reveal them earlier;
- contract variation and procurement change orders;
- effectiveness of procedures for acceptance and hand-over;
- level of customer satisfaction achieved;
- soundness of cash flows and liability control;
- forecast profit and actual profit;
- relevant recommendations for improvement of company procedures for the management of projects.

4.9 Risk portfolio

4.9.1 Introduction

The term Risk Portfolio is used in the *RISKMAN* Methodology to describe collated risk data assembled for the management of the project.

An extensive collection of forms and standard documents has been developed to assist in assembling the risk database. Some of these forms have been used to illustrate the text of this book. The suitability of specific formats varies for given organisations and even of individual projects within any one organisation. Tailoring is usually necessary to a greater or lesser degree, dependant on the risk management maturity of the organisation, and individuals involved, and the level of the methodology which is to be applied.

The preceding chapters, in describing the *RISKMAN* Methodology, have emphasised that risks have many attributes and relationships that enables them to be sorted, prioritised and managed.

To assist in the administration of the risk database the relevant data may be stored in a database (which may or may not be a computer database), in a format and manner which will enable the risks to be accessed, or brought to the attention of the functional managers that form the project team.

Risks are also prioritised for management and reporting purposes, and reports collated to correspond with these needs.

In the paragraphs below the minimum information that needs to be contained in the risk database will be described.

4.9.2 *RISKMAN* risk requirements summary

The *RISKMAN* methodology requires:

- that all risks are uniquely identified and described;
- that care is taken to include consequential risks and combinations of risks;
- risk to be assessed for likelihood (probability) of occurrence and potential impact on the programme, cost or performance;
- all non-cost impacts to be calculated out on their cost implications;
- each major risk to have a mitigation strategy;
- major risks to be assigned a trigger event in the project programme;

- each risk to have an owner responsible for its management;
- each risk to be related to the event that it effects in the WBS, the OBS and CBS as appropriate;
- risk to be prioritised;
- risks to be reviewed at regular intervals;
- risk status to be reported at regular intervals;
- a risk model to be developed, that contains all the uncertainties and risk estimates that may effect the programme timescales or costs;
- risk contingencies to be identified against the event that will incur the risk;
- subcontractors to be assessed for risks;
- risk management plans to be in place.

4.10 Computer support for risk management

There are no specific mandatory requirements that stipulate that computers are essential for risk management. In fact many companies that successfully implement risk management as part of their culture do not use computers for the risk management process.

Computers do, however, enable large amounts of information to be processed and manipulated in a relatively short time period. They enable calculations to be accurately performed and outputs to be produced to meet the reporting and management needs of others. They are also capable of taking in information from remote positions and transmitting it to others, as and when required, or requested. Computers can therefore make the management of data more acceptable and speed up the processing, factors which make them attractive and useful tools for risk management.

In risk management computers are used for the following activities:

- storing the risk database;
- assessing and analysing the risks;
- performing the calculations for risk factor and decision-making;
- sorting the information into the required outputs as previously described;
- printing out risk registers and risk summaries;
- running risk models;

- predicting the effect of risks;
- running expert systems and knowledge-based systems;
- calculating risk contingencies;
- producing project reports;
- producing statistics on effectiveness of risk management.

Because of their versatility, computer systems can produce risk reports in many different formats to suit the individualism of the project's functional managers.

The *RISKMAN* methodology requires that the risks be stored under twelve categories or risk areas. It is also essential to store the information so that it may be retrieved by work area and individual responsibility.

In a large project there may be many work areas and a great many subcontractors (e.g. Channel Tunnel; Nuclear Submarine Construction). On a very large project they may run into a few thousand, though only a few hundred may be major. It follows therefore that if the risks are to be stored and processed on a large project, a computer becomes essential just to manage the data. The project model will require a computer to carry out the many calculations that are necessary to obtain a reasonable certainty in the predictions of exposure in timescales and costs. During the contract's execution it would be expeditious to use a computer to obtain predictions arising from changes to the programme and to the risks.

Expert systems are likely to offer real opportunities to extend the effectiveness of risk management support in the next few years. At this point in time however, such systems are still in their infancy.

Most computer-based software systems used for risk management will run satisfactorily on a desk-top personal computer (PC). The largest single problem in using PCs in the past has been interfacing with other computers, in particular those running the project programme and/or the financial cost estimating system; no system should be purchased for risk management without the ability to interchange data with these key corporate systems.

Most computer software for risk management is actually aimed at applying statistical techniques to modelling risk. This can be very valid and useful. However, such an exhaustive approach is applicable in relatively few scenarios in real life. For the day-to-day management of project risk, it is possible to get a great deal more value from standard software tools such as spreadsheets, database systems and word processors, combined with an understanding of what is needed to gain effective management control of risk.

Indeed, for very small projects, effective risk management can be administered with no more than a word processor.

Since the use of a methodology for risk management has previously been restricted to a few select areas such as defence projects, it is not surprising that there is little software developed specifically for this purpose. It is to be hoped that this situation will change rapidly, and this has been a major motivation for the publication of *RISKMAN*. A major output of the *RISKMAN* initiative will take the form of computerised support for risk management, and the documented methodology is intended to provide the specification for such developments.

4.11 Capturing corporate risk experience

Corporate experience is locked into a company's history files and in the reasons and thinking that goes into decision-making by its staff. All too often the reasons and thinking exist only in the memories of individuals. The effectiveness of decisions taken, or otherwise, and the reasons for modifying them during the project life-cycle, can only be determined if the results are recorded and analysed. Inadequate recording of the reasons for taking decisions that increase or decrease risk exposure, and in the reporting of progress, results in corporate experience being lost.

Sound risk management at all *RISKMAN* levels of implementation requires that recording of corporate experience is enforced through the establishment of a project history file. Such a file contains, as a minimum, the following:

- Board of Directors memos and minutes of Directors meetings, or extracts from them, that record decisions taken that affect the project, and the reasons for them;
- The proposal and/or contract specification as finally agreed;
- Contract terms and conditions as finally agreed;
- Contract variation orders;
- Project cost estimates at initial bid stage; as used in final contract; as revised (if any) at project start-up;
- Project risk status summaries;
- Project financial reports;
- Project programme reports from project team members to project manager;
- Project Manager's status reports;
- Minutes of all project meetings including risk review meetings;

- The minutes of the Project Director's reviews of the project;
- Minutes of meetings with customer;
- Project audit reports;
- Project management and control procedures as in force during the project;
- Project Manager's project completion report.

Some of the documents in the list above are primarily concerned with the recording of decisions and the reasons for them, that may change the perspective of the project risks. Such decisions may take the form of:

authorisation for the release of the proposal to the customer;

decision to reduce the risk contingency fund or remove all profits;

decision to initiate a project audit when concern is expressed that the project is not achieving its performance;

decision to enter a teaming or joint venture arrangement that will affect the project;

decision to reduce the price and invest in capital expenditure for some item of the project;

decision to change the resources available to the project manager;

decision to no-bid a project.

One of the project manager's most important jobs is the management of the client (in the case of programmes management, this function may be assumed by the programme manager, but he should liaise with the project manager on all items that are discussed affecting the project). The project manager is likely to be at, or send a representative to all meetings concerning the project with the client. However, directors and higher level managers or marketing and sales staff may also attend many meetings with the customer and partners in the project, that reveal or may create risks to the success of the project. Such information, where it can be appropriately released to the project manager, should form an entry in the project history file.

The authorisation to release the proposal to the customer may take the form of an approval sign-off sheet that authorises the price to be tendered. In some cases it may also authorise the negotiating margins and contain instructions for actions to be taken under certain circumstances should they arise. Such a sign-off sheet forms an essential part of the history file.

The proposal, when up-dated at the start of the project, forms the initial basis for the project plan. The proposal is therefore an essential part of the project's history and will be used to assess the success or otherwise of the project on completion.

All of the remaining documents listed above are directly in the control of the project manager. The prime function of these documents is to facilitate project audits and the production of the Project Close Down Report. It is also a fact that should any dispute arise on the performance of the contract then these files form an essential part of the record of the work that was undertaken.

4.12 Decisions and approvals

The final decisions and approvals to accept risk exposure, or to increase or decrease the risk exposure must be made by higher management. Such decisions cannot be taken lightly. They may involve the abandonment of considerable expenditure on marketing when a no-bid decision is made.

On committing the company to future high risk activity it follows that the information provided must include clear data on all major risks and evidence that the project has been thoroughly researched for all risks.

It is essential that clear guidelines and rules are provided to project management teams on how higher management require risk information presented, and what other supporting data is required, to assist in making decisions.

Figure 3.24 is an example of how the price build-up information can be presented and Figure 4.3 illustrates how the spread of the major risks can be shown. This need requires that higher management put in place standard overheads and profit margins and risk assessment and calculation procedures, so that all proposals are presented without adjustments and with no hidden contingency at the bid team level.

It follows that if adjustments are to be allowed, the rules for such adjustments must be clearly identified. For example; if a bid is to be subsidised then the source of the subsidy must be identified for when things do go wrong.

Some examples of such rules are as follows:

- If capital expenditure is required to support the proposal then this must be clearly identified.

- If any single risk exposure exceeds the approved profit margin then it must be separately identified together with its mitigation strategy.

- If the proposal requires a joint venture or acquisition then approval must be sought in advance of establishing the relationship.

- There must be a sufficiently high chance of achieving the standard profit margin.

- There must be no hidden subsidies within the estimates.

- Adjustments to the proposal price estimate must not be made without the prior approval of higher management, (Financial Director/Managing Director).

All companies allocate approval levels to appropriate grades of staff, who are then in a position to approve risk exposure and expenditure up to the limits of their approval authority. However risks are created if the rules do not ensure that the appropriate departments are involved in the decision making process. An example of such a rule is: *The Finance Department must be consulted concerning any bid proposal that requires the buying forward of foreign currency.*

It also follows that the project manager must consult with all appropriate departments when risks are identified that require such departments to become involved in the mitigation or risk management activity. When seeking approvals all departments must be involved in the risk appraisal activity at least to the extent of recording a none or minimum risk report so that their involvement is to be seen.

Under the above circumstance it follows that a standard set of documentation to support a decision by higher management must be prepared by the appropriate departments and brought together by the project manager, in support of the price and proposal documentation. Such documentation needs to be carefully defined, and tight procedures enforced to ensure its completion.

To assist in reaching these decisions, several techniques are available including:

- the decision tree which enables the evaluation of a set of scenarios, and to make a comparison of them according to a set of pre-defined criteria (highs, lows, most acceptable, etc.);

- the multi-criteria chart which provides a (limited) list of fundamental questions in order to summarise a situation (see Figure 4.16);

- market analysis by using standard techniques such as those presented in the literature (Boston Consulting Group). An example is given in Figure 4.17.

The purpose of such analyses is to decide whether to continue or stop an activity by focusing on a reduced set of fundamental elements to its success.

Criterion	Scenario 1	Scenario 2	Scenario 3
Risk budget			
Synergy with other activities			
Return on investment timing			
Re-usable know-how			
Costs due to new type of business			
New market			
Competition			

Figure 4.16 Example of multi-criteria chart

Market position	Start	Growing	Mature	Decrease
Dominant				
High				
Medium				
Marginal				

Figure 4.17 Example market analysis chart

5
Risk-Driven Project Management Process

This chapter examines the principle of managing a project from a risk perception. Given that all projects are risk prone to some degree, we will consider the repeated operation of the risk management cycle during the various phases of the project.

An awareness of the potential of risk to fundamentally impact upon the outcome of a project will dictate a risk-driven strategy for managing projects, which may be significantly different to that which would be applied if the risk was not apparent.

We will consider responsibility for both the process of managing risk and for individual risks as one moves through the project cycle. The interaction of risk exposure with the size, complexity and organisational constraints of the project will indicate the level of detail which is desirable for risk management activity. *RISKMAN* has identified general levels of application, but there are no hard barriers to divide these levels. We will examine different sizes and types of project and relate variation in risk management to them.

The *RISKMAN* methodology prescribes an approach to risk management which influences all phases of a project and therefore determines that project management should embody the process of managing risk in all phases of the project. We will examine the risk management activity which should take place in each of these phases. The effects of incorporating *RISKMAN* in the management of the various aspects of a project, together with its impact upon the project management organisation, will be explored.

The conclusion drawn from this chapter has to be that the effective management of projects is only possible with the adoption of a satisfactory approach to the analysis and management of risk. Such an approach will determine the philosophy, and define the strategy for the management of any project.

5.1 Changing roles, responsibilities and ownership

One could take the point of view that a project is at risk irrespective of the circumstances under which it is realised. The evolving circumstances of a project's planning and execution not only change the nature and degree of risk, but one's perspective of the risk. If one adopts this philosophy, then it becomes obvious that risk identification and control is a fundamental function, which should be performed throughout every stage of any project.

Risk management is not merely a *damage limitation* exercise to protect those who execute the project from "the slings and arrows of outrageous fortune". It should be directed to creating an environment in which the project, itself, is protected from any threat which has the potential to prevent the realisation of that project's objective.

Of course a project's objectives may be different, or at least perceived to be different, depending upon the attitude of that organisation which bears the principal responsibility for the project, at the various stages of its realisation.

For instance, when the project is being conceptualised only one objective may be apparent - for example that of acquiring the technical desiderata - in which case any risk analysis activity will be focused upon limiting the potential for that objective to be compromised. At a later stage in the development of the concept, the questions of price and delivery may become more significant, and attract more attention in terms of risk management.

When the project is being realised, during the execution phase, the actual provision of a technical solution should be less of an issue. But the consequence of technical difficulties upon one's ability to provide that solution, within defined cost and schedule limitations, will certainly attract a great deal of attention and be the principle focus of one's risk management efforts.

Whatever the focus, and method, of risk analysis, risk control is a constant requirement throughout the life of a project. In the same way that a project needs to be managed throughout its life, and that function is fulfilled by a variety of authorities - depending upon the maturity of its development, risk aspects of the project also need to be managed. This philosophy leads one to the belief that managing project risks is an intrinsic function of managing the project.

Of course, whilst risk management may be a constant requirement, the means by which one evaluates risk - in order to be able to exercise control - depends upon one's perspective of the project's objectives and its maturity, in terms of development.

5.2 Variation with type and size of project

The methods that one would employ and the degree to which those methods would be employed to manage a project, differ depending upon the demands of both the project and the organisation undertaking the project. The same thing applies to risk management. It has already been stated that a coherent approach to risk management is an intrinsic component of an effective project management philosophy, and it therefore follows that the degree to which risk management is applied to a project situation is dictated by the need.

Large, complex projects can be expected to be more risk prone that others. One should expect, therefore, to need to be more rigorous and perhaps more analytical, in one's approach to managing the risk aspects of the project.

Of course, even relatively small projects can be inherently risk prone. In which case, perhaps one should consider an assessment of a project's propensity, or potential, to be risk prone.

Unfortunately, this is not as straightforward as one may expect. The assessment may be more dependent upon the attitude and ability of the organisation which is to execute the project, than on the characteristics of the project itself. This is probably why purchasing authorities are now tending to require suppliers to formally assess the degree of risk in a project. That assessment tells the purchaser more about suppliers' attitudes to project risks than any performance analysis could do.

In other chapters of this book, we attempt to draw a correlation between the demands of a project, for risk management, and the capacity of an organisation to undertake risk management. This correlation will tend to indicate the degree, or level, to which *RISKMAN* methods need to be adopted. It is, of course, somewhat subjective and difficult to formalise.

There is no doubt that every project, irrespective of its size or complexity, requires administration of the risk aspects. This need not be a burdensome activity. It is after all just sound project management!

The minimum requirement is that all potential risks are identified and classified. This may require a certain level of cause and effect analysis to be carried out (see Appendix C2). It is of great advantage to then consider the probable impact of these risks upon the project. Qualitative prioritisation can be of great benefit at this stage, and is an extremely effective and simple method of ranking project risks (see Appendix C1). From this exercise, there will be indications of how the more significant risks should be addressed. One may then consider a variety of methods and techniques to, more objectively, quantify risks and their impacts, if that approach was found to be necessary or even of benefit.

This exercise, of course, merely indicates the potential level of effort needed to effectively manage, within the province of project management, the risk aspects of the project. How that level of effort should be utilised would depend upon the classification of the risk. For instance, one may consider that a technical risk could be eliminated at some cost, by employing a different method of manufacture.

Principally, strategies for the mitigation of risk, perhaps to the point of elimination, should be considered before resorting to the creation and inflation of a risk budget, but when a risk cannot be sufficiently mitigated, the potential occurrence of that risk must then be budgeted for. A simple spreadsheet approach to probabilistic analysis (see Appendix C) is an adequate method for aggregating a risk budget.

The creation of a risk budget is the source of another management perspective for the project manager. He or she will become responsible for the stewardship of that budget - managing the project with its inherent risk elements so as to preserve as much of the risk budget as possible. The risk budget may be a significant source, for some the only source, of potential profit.

For many projects, a highly sophisticated approach to the analysis and quantification of risk is, perhaps, an unnecessarily complex and costly procedure. For all project activity, a systematic and diligent assessment of risk is essential and need not be either complex or expensive.

5.3 Conceptual or pre-bid phase

In chapter 4 the three main stages of a project were identified commencing with the pre-bid phase, and in Figure 4.8 the activities required of the project management team were summarised.

Figure 3.28 shows risk-driven project management as a process that embodies good project management practice with the risk management process illustrated in Figure 3.23. The risk management process is repeated at every stage in a project life-cycle so that a continuity and growing assessment of risk to success are obtained. This is shown in Figure 5.1.

During the conceptual or pre-bid phase when the marketing/sales staff are seeking new orders, the project and other functional departments are working in a marketing/sales support role.

During this period relationships with potential customers are established and a start is made on determining the most likely means of realising a contract from this relationship. New products are under development aimed at meeting future market requirements.

Preliminary negotiations are commenced with potential risk sharing or key skills and technology owning partners and preliminary outlines of potential solutions, to the customer's and market's perceived requirements, are prepared.

Repeated at every stage in the project life-cycle

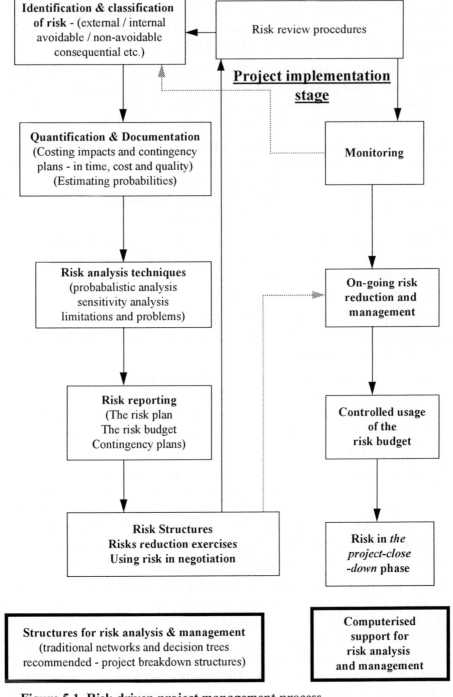

Figure 5.1 Risk-driven project management process

It has been stated earlier, that risks start from day one of a project's life. It takes but little thought to realise that in developing relationships with customers, future risks to success may be created through the company's capabilities being over sold and the customers' expectations having been raised beyond that which can be achieved in reality.

Developing early relationships with potential partners is also just as likely to create risks. Each potential partner will endeavour to protect their market and negotiating positions as well as their knowledge and capabilities until the relationship is sealed, and to a degree, even beyond this point.

Business relationships are also formed for strategic reasons, such as obtaining a larger share of the market and not just for one project, which may lead to different risks. Potential partners may have both open and hidden agendas and commitments may be entered that cannot be changed, should they prove unsuitable for a particular project, at a later date.

Company commitments made at the outset of business, through marketing forecasts and product sales, also change if the market and sales fail to reach expectations. Funding for products and projects may be reduced and resources committed to alternative markets.

The identification and management of risks in the pre-bid phase are extremely important and if not soundly approached may lead to failure to win or to successfully implement a project.

It follows from the above that if the project manager is to be responsible for winning and implementation of a project then it is necessary for the project department to be fully involved in the pre-bid discussions and negotiations, and that procedures are in place to assist in the identification, assessment and mitigation of risks.

The *RISKMAN* project risk management methodology requires that risks are addressed at every phase in a project's life-cycle. This means that the requirements of the *RISKMAN* methodology must be embedded in the company's business instructions and procedures, and that managers be made responsible for keeping the project manager aware of their activities and decisions that may create risks to the success of the project in the future.

Within the risk management process in Chapter 4 we discussed the pre-bid activities and identified that key to successful risk management is the identification of the risks. A number of alternative methods for identifying risks were introduced and the limitations of each identified. Companies are successful in their line of business because they have developed a culture that meets the market requirements. This culture must also be re-assessed to determine how risk management can be introduced to the benefit of the company.

Successful risk management requires information to be more openly provide to those capable of identifying and mitigating the risks. A major concern to most companies is the distribution of business information and customer status information down (and in some cases up) through management levels where it may inadvertently be revealed to competitors. Since the success of a company is equally important to its employees, it follows that the release of business information to them must be managed as well as protected, however sufficient detail must be provided to enable risks to be identified.

Each stage in a project life-cycle is generally supported in a company by reporting forms and for the pre-bid phase these may comprise forms such as Initial Inquiries Status Reports or Negotiation Opening Reports. Whatever the title of such forms they do provide a means for informing senior management of the commencement of new business equating to the start of new risks.

It is at this stage that the project history file should commence. It is recognised that a project or risk manager may not have been appointed. However, the history file can be started by the commercial or marketing/sales managers ready for transfer to the project manager when appointed. These forms provide a useful method for advising the potential risk owners of the possible existence of new risks.

If the professional management of risk is to be achieved, the risk management process must be embedded into company business practice. This requires that all persons involved in developing new business must be educated and trained to operate this stage of the risk management process. From this point on they must be kept informed of the status of the project and must have a means for having their concerns/risks addressed. If the project manager is not yet in place, special mechanisms need to be established to cope with the situation.

Business practice must be assessed by looking carefully at the role that the project manager or project manager designate can play in managing the risks at this early stage. Full involvement in the early stages of negotiations enables the project manager to bring his experience in managing risk into play early. It enables him to act as a focal point within the company for all persons involved or likely to be involved in the project at a later date. Risks can be investigated and information provided to the marketing sales teams on what needs to be done to mitigate them. Senior management can be informed of the risks and receive supporting information to assist in negotiations with potential partners to minimise the chance of risks being built into future relationships. This is a complex subject which cannot be fully addressed here. However, in the majority of projects that go badly wrong, the causes of the problems were built in to the scenario taken over by the project manager. They were created at this point before he arrived.

Many companies will say that they already do these things and still risks are not being identified. The main reason why is generally the lack of a risk management culture. Risks are hidden or played down. Staff are not aware of how risks are created or what constitutes a risk. Staff are informed of the potential new business, but with insufficient information to identify potential risks, there is no means provided for them to input into the business process. Marketing/Sales managers are too busy to prepare detailed briefs, or the negotiations are classified as too sensitive to involve others for the purpose of preventing interference.

Management do not wish to have the constraints of informing others of their activities or decisions until they have completed the process and do not appreciate the huge gains from doing so. They are reluctant to document the reasons for their decisions leading to a loss of corporate knowledge.

The mitigation of risks during the pre-bid stage primarily revolves around putting into place strategies that will reduce the risk at some time in the future. Some of the early risks are company-owned risks, that involve obtaining commitment to proceed to another phase of the project. Being open about the risks involved can give rise to concerns over obtaining such commitment. A phrase that occurs in risk management is the *'thrill of the chase'*. This phrase is used to cover the actions taken by the marketing/sales and later the bid/proposal team to achieve their desired aim, even if this means ignoring potential risks or creating risks by hiding unpleasant facts from senior management. Senior management must create an atmosphere of being open about risks and taking decisions based on assessments of risks if this attitude is to be alleviated.

Senior management are responsible for the acceptance of risk exposure on behalf of a company, it therefore follows that senior management must be the leader in creating and implementing a risk management culture within the project management process. The project manager is responsible for control of the risk management process involving the flow of information to those concerned either to identify or to mitigate the risks. It is a project management function to prepare the project risk assessment that should accompany any request to senior management for funding and approval to continue with the pre-bid activities or to enter the bidphase.

5.4 Initial planning or bid phase

The initial planning or bid phase concerns those activities involved in preparing a proposal and price to comply with a customer's requirements. It also includes those activities concerned with obtaining approval to release the proposal to the customer and negotiation of the contract.

The activities that the project manager must implement to realise the project can be summarised as Analysis, Estimate, Organise, and Follow-up. These high-level activities have been explained in Chapter 3 and are shown in Figure 5.2 in relationship to the contractual and technical processes.

Analyse	•Preliminary Breakdown Structure (WBS)	•Precise WBS •Value Analysis	•Final WBS •Risks	•Evolutions and Changes	•WBS Updates for production constraints	• Changes	•Evolutions and Changes
Estimate	•Draft Estimates	•Precise Estimates	•Final Development Estimates	•Final Production Cost Estimates	•Deployment Costs	•Maintenance Costs	•Evolution Cost
Organise	•Master Plan	•Detailed Plan & Updated Master Plan	•Plan Committed	•Re-scheduling •Production Plan	•Deployment Plan •Maintenance	•Setting to Work	•Maintenance Plan
Follow-up				•Progress Controls •C&E Control	•Productivity Control •C & E Control	•C & E Control	•Age of Spare Parts •Stocks •C & E Control

Contractual Process	Pre-Bid	Bid	Negotiation	Project Execution Period			Warranty Period

Technical Process	Need Analysis & Feasibility	Development	Production	Deployment			Maintenance

Figure 5.2 Project activity related to contractual/technical processes

The risk management activity in the bid-phase generally commences with receipt of an Invitation to Tender (ITT)/Request for Proposal (RFP)/Request for Quotation (RFQ). It may commence earlier if sufficient details of the customer's requirements are available to enable a proposal response to be formed. In the case of products or small value contracts it may commence with receipt of a letter requesting a proposal to quote for the supply of the product or services. The information on the customer's actual requirements up to this point will, in general, be incomplete. In the case of an internal project, the phase commences as soon as management ask someone to document a formal proposal.

The *RISKMAN* methodology requires that any risk assessments up to this point be re-assessed in the light of current information. Should the risk exposure have changed adversely from that previously forecast by the project manager during the pre-bid phase, then approval should be sought to continue with the bid process or to confirm a no-bid decision.

A no-bid decision is a risk reduction path: many companies are reluctant to make such a decision, particularily after having established relationships with the customer and potential partners. The perceived image of the company and its reputation in the market place and future business relationships with the customer are considered to be at risk. A decision to no-bid is therefore never taken lightly. The scenario for this path should have been set during the pre-bid phase, external commitments should be restricted to those that fully meet the company's strategic intentions, level of commitment authorised and risk management capabilities.

Refusing to bid can harm the company's relationship with the customer. Very often a *no-bid* decision is implemented in practice by the company deliberately submitting a proposal, which they believe will be unacceptable, and doing so at minimum cost. This can have a hidden danger. The company does not want to submit a proposal which is ludicrously priced or badly non-compliant, because that might harm its reputation more than refusing to bid. Therefore the company puts in what it considers to be a reasonable, but slightly high-priced bid. It does not spend much money considering the bid, and certainly does not spend much on a professional and detailed risk analysis. Most project companies have won the occasional contract this way, when they did not expect or intend to win. All too often they find out why they won when they come to the detailed planning stage and start to uncover all those nasty things they overlooked when the RFQ came in. They should have done a risk analysis after all, and it was a false economy to submit a bid prepared at minimum cost.

The process of risk management in the bid-phase commences with a detailed analysis of the RFQ documentation by a multi-functional team commensurate with the level of technical and commercial documentation received from the customer. On a small proposal or in a small company the team may comprise one man, for example the project or estimating manager. For a major project, the team may comprise a large number of staff members representing every functional department and be augmented by potential risk sharing or subcontractors' personnel.

The project manager/risk manager/project manager designate should lead the team in reading through the RFQ documentation and identifying potential risk areas. All risks that are identified must be recorded and an initial assessment made of their probability and impact. This initial assessment can then be used to identify those areas where mitigation strategies should be investigated.

On a small project, at this stage, a considerable amount of information on the risks will be available, perhaps in sufficient detail to enable the risk identification process to be terminated. However, it may be necessary to continue the process by a more detailed planning of the project and development of a potential design solution to finalise the risk identification process.

On a large project sufficient information will be available to terminate some of the risk identification processes, e.g. risks in most of the categorisation classes with the exception of process, product, operational or maintenance will be known in great detail. Exceptions such as those mentioned will only be known in outline until the project is planned and a proposed technical solution developed.

It is necessary for the project management team to understand the entire project process and the inter-relationship of events in order to effectively identify the risk elements, to identify and provide monitor risk triggers and to develop decision networks for mitigating risk elements.

Relationships between the risk element, the risk triggers, and the programme milestones potentially impacted by the risk must be developed in order to effectively plan mitigation decisions.

The project manager is responsible for planning the programme in sufficient detail to enable the relationships mentioned above to be developed by the project management team. The project manager must also breakdown the work in a structured manner and develop the organisation that will be needed to implement the project.

The project manager has a number of tools available to assist in planning the work, including requirements analysis tools, work breakdown structures (WBS), and organisation breakdown structures (OBS); he must also be guided by the needs and constraints of the activities and the organisation.

A structured approach is therefore taken within project management and adapted in applying risk management similar to the concurrent engineering approach that is used in technical departments. A model of the activities can be constructed to indicate how the constraints relate; Figure 3.31 shows a typical high-level model used in constraints analysis.

The Technical (Engineering/Operations/Support) organisations under the authority of the project manager will conduct the necessary development work on the technical requirements by using methods such as requirements analysis, Functional Breakdown Structure (FBS), or Product Breakdown Structure (PBS) trade-off studies and Logistic Support Analysis (LSA) to arrive at a proposed solution and alternatives to meet the customer's technical requirements.

For a prime contractorship arrangement, much of the technical organisation's work will be conducted by subcontractors, the management of which will also create risks.

The scenario for the project is now established and enables a more detailed examination of the work activities for risks, with the following items now being available :

- customers requirements analysis report(s);
- work breakdown structure (WBS);
- organisation breakdown structure (OBS);
- initial overall programme of activities;
- technical solution and/or alternatives;
- quality/performance specifications;
- acceptance requirements;
- logistics support requirements.

Because most of the work in arriving at the above is specialist in nature, the project manager must select, for the culture in which he works, the most appropriate, method or a combination of the methods described in Section 4.1.1 to identify the risks.

Assuming that it is proposed to use structured interviewing techniques, the project manager (or risk manager on a large project) will arrange to interview the lead specialist in each of the organisations functional work areas to identify the risks and to relate these to the WBS. The use of prepared discussion material and risk questionnaires will assist this process.

Whether or not structured interviewing or brainstorming and/or checklists are used for risk identification, cost estimating forms should **always** make provision for risk identification during the estimating task, or be supplemented by separate risk identification forms.

This has the advantage of each area being responsible for documenting the existence of the risks. It is also likely to indicate where additional interviews need to be conducted with the risk owners to clarify some of the information provided.

The risk information now available to the project manager will enable a detailed assessment of the risks in the project to be conducted. Each risk can then be assessed and prioritised and mitigation planned and/or implemented for those risks with a medium to high risk factor.

Subcontractors will have been issued with requests for proposals (RFPs) accompanied by a statement of work and/or a technical specification covering their activities. Included within this must, of course, be the need for them to identify any risks that will affect the project programme and/or deliverables. Their proposals and prices will be made available for assessment and selection so that they can be incorporated into the price estimate being prepared for the customer.

This enables the bid manager to provide to the price estimators sufficient details of the risks that require to be entered into the cost estimates and to relate these to the WBS and subcontractors activities. At this stage the bid team can prepare the price estimates and supporting documentation that is required to obtain a decision from higher management on whether or not to release the proposal and price to the customer.

This is an exit stage for the company, if the financial risk exposure is considered to be too great, that it has moved adversely from that previously reported, and the risks are unmanageable, then a no-bid decision may be entered. It is however, also a period of negotiation with team members and subcontractors to further reduce the risks and price estimate. It is also the time when senior management must decide the acceptable level of risk exposure taking into consideration factors such as:

- importance of project/product to company strategic aims;
- financial effects of continuing with the project;
- effect of project cancellation on other existing or anticipated projects, or the programme within which the project fits;
- the view of the market/customer should the company fail to continue with the project;
- the chances of winning at the estimated price;
- the need for capital investment.

With a go decision and an approved level of financial risk exposure, the final price estimate can be prepared and the proposal and price released to the customer. The risk contingency budget may have been adjusted and this adjustment must be taken into account by the project manager by relating the adjustment down to the contingency estimates for subcontractors and internal WBS items.

On a small project, or in a small company, the above factors and any changes may be very easy to relate; the approvals activity may even be conducted at the same desk where the price estimate is prepared and the only factor that needs considering may be, "Can we win at this price?"

The activities now change as the proposal, prices and technical specification are provided to the customer, and negotiations commence.

For a small value proposal with limited technical content the negotiations may take the form of an acceptance or rejection. If any clarification is entered it may take the form of a letter or telephone call. The validity period of the proposal will probably be short and the customer will most likely be aware of the risks involved in the activity.

For a high value proposal with a major technical content and a programme that extents over a considerable time period, the customer will most likely enter a prolonged period of proposal evaluation and clarification.

The *RISKMAN* methodology requires the project manager to establish a procedure for handling queries as they arise and to involve the risk owners including subcontractors in the preparation of responses. The price on the table is negotiable and the customer is aware of this. The risk exposure can be changed adversely in preparing the responses to the customer's queries, subcontractors may not have included for the work they say will be done in responses, and it is the responsibility of the project manager to ensure that any increase in risk falls within the negotiating margins or is contained within existing risk contingencies, both of which may be under attack from the customer.

The proposed contract terms and conditions may also be subjected to the clarification activity, conditions that the company may have rejected will be queried by the customer and any risks that the company have proposed should be retained by the customer (the avoidance path) to affect a price reduction will be open to negotiation.

The initial planning and bid phase activity is completed when the above negotiations are terminated by acceptance or rejection of the amended estimates and proposal contents.

5.5 Implementation Phase

The implementation phase may commence with receipt of a letter of intent to proceed (ITP) or a contract, arising from the completion of negotiations. At this stage the company may decide not to proceed further with the project, a decision that cannot be taken lightly by the company that by now may have expended much of its marketing budget on achieving the contract. However, this is likely to be the final exit point open to senior management before the risk exposure becomes totally unacceptable due to the penalty conditions that would be imposed by acceptance of the contract.

The project manager may not have the authority to accept the contract on behalf of the company (acceptance of the risk); however, he does need to be involved in the decision process. A decision to accept a contract's existence, based on the ITP, could prove disastrous if the contract is delayed and liabilities entered into without a capability to fully recover the expenditure should the contract fail to materialise or contain unacceptable conditions.

The final contract terms and conditions may have been amended after the agreements reached during negotiations and the need may exist to clarify the final contract terms and conditions with the customer before proceeding.

In the *RISKMAN* methodology it is essential for the company to have procedures in place for the acceptance of contracts and ITPs that will enable the risks in acceptance to be identified and where necessary, appropriate action put into effect to reduce/control them.

Following acceptance of the contract or authorisation to proceed, the project manager must initiate a re-evaluation of the bid/proposal documentation to incorporate any changes that may now be required to arrive at a full specification for the job. The bid price estimates must be adjusted to take account of any changes that have taken place, and new levels of risk budgets assigned to the work breakdown elements.

The baseline contract specification[18] will, for the future, only be changed under a formal contract change-control environment. From this point, should the customer wish to initiate a change to the requirement, or the company determines that the specification needs amendment, then a formal contract change procedure (contract variation order) should be in place. The procedure and format for such changes should be stated in the contract.

Subcontractor's statements of work and process may need re-working to reflect the changes. Orders must be placed with due consideration of the future liabilities that may arise should the subcontractor's risk assessments process prove to have been less than thorough.

RISKMAN requires that the project manager reviews the resource allocations and the OBS and seeks to have the appropriate staff assigned to commence the work. Confirmation/instructions should be prepared and issued to the appropriate departments together with the current project programme, WBS, OBS and appropriate budget authorisations (CBS)[19].

The risks assessments carried out during the bid phase must now be re-assessed by the implementation team to determine their status and, if required, mitigation activities may be re-planned to take account of the current status of the project and revised knowledge obtained during negotiations.

The project manager must initiate a review of the project and project risk status and report to higher management at regular intervals. The project status report would incorporate the risk summary produced from the risk

---

[18]Dependent on the project environment and type of project, *specification* may here mean either *product specification* or *requirements specification*.

[19]Dependent on the financial system in place, the CBS may obviate the necessity of publishing a separate OBS.

register, the statistics associated with the number of risks in the database and the effectiveness of implementation strategies.

The project manager is required to ensure that the project team, including subcontractors, report on the status of current and imminent risks at each status review. Any new risks that are belatedly identified are also reported and subjected to the same assessment process as were risks already in the risk register. The project budget should include a financial contingency to cover residual risk exposure. If changes in risk exposure identified at project reviews threaten to exceed the contingency allowed, the project manager must report this to senior management. He needs clear guidelines as to when such reporting is expected and through which channels.

During the course of the project, configuration management (evolution control) must be strictly enforced if risks are not to be created by persons using outdated information, systems or equipment, through being unaware of the current status. Two particularly critical areas are drawing and software control.

The project manager, in implementing project risk management, can measure his effectiveness by the level of benefit that he can report as being achieved through completion of risky activities with minimal or no occurrence of the risks. The risk contingency that is not spent can of course be used by the project manager to assist in alleviating the spend on more difficult risks or to fund the resolution of *new* risks as they are identified.

RISKMAN recognises that there is inaccuracy and uncertainty in the main plan for the project, so there can be overspend and/or underspend against that, and there is likely to be a need for a budgetary allowance to cover such overspend. Some companies may attempt to separate the budgetary allowances for such uncertainty from their budgetary allowance for the uncertainty associated with risk occurrences which cause changes to main plan. *RISKMAN* does not specify either approach as being more desirable. However, it should be noted that, on the odd occasion when things go well in the main plan, that it is likely to be desirable to utilise unused time and/or budget to bolster the risk allocation.

At the end of the project, any unused fiscal risk allocation becomes additional profit. With long duration projects lasting several years, it may be desirable to release unused risk allocation, to profit during the life of the project. However, this practice can be very dangerous and should be embarked upon with great care. Whilst the *RISKMAN* methodology can again not be specific concerning how much to release and when, the *RISKMAN* manuals will allocate significant space to advice the project manager who is pressurised to release risk budget to profit prematurely.

On major projects it is necessary to review the risks in the database and the risk register at regular intervals. The project manager must assign a Risk Review Team to carry out this review (see Chapter 4).

The project manager is also required to provide regular reports on the financial status of the project including the status of risk contingency spend and liabilities. This report which is an essential element of the project status report enables senior management to determine the effectiveness of the project risk management.

Significant change will be experienced in the risk portfolio as it progresses through its implementation phase. This will be the case regardless of the thoroughness with which initial risk identification and risk planning has been implemented. Some risks initially considered to be no more than *areas of concern* will become significant. Some risks initially considered to be highly significant will become unimportant. New risks will turn up which are very significant, but were not even identified in the initial analysis activity. These new risks were not unforeseeable, but they were unforeseen. None of this invalidates the genuine benefit of implementing a structured and disciplined approach to risk analysis and control. In cases where a pro-active risk management culture has been established, the project team has been prepared to face the challenges of the implementation phase, and will generally succeed.

The project manager must maintain the project history file. Should a need be determined for the project to be audited, either by the project manager or by higher management, or by the arrival of an appropriate milestone in the programme, it is this history file which will be used to determine risk management effectiveness within the project.

A project audit must be initiated within the early months of a project's implementation, to establish a baseline and confirm that the project risks are being managed appropriately. On a large programme, the audit may be repeated at annual intervals. However, audits can be initiated by higher management whenever it can be shown that concerns over the status of the project are sufficiently valid to warrant such an audit.

Irrespective of the level of *RISKMAN* being implemented by the company, the success of its risk management can only be determined by monitoring the effectiveness of its mitigation plans as measured by the level of contingency spend and liabilities outstanding against the original forecasts provided at the start of the project.

5.6 Project phase-out and whole-life activities

At project completion, the effectiveness of risk management and of the bid estimating process can be determined by analysis of the project history file. This analysis is carried out by the project manager and the implementation functional managers, by evaluating the data in the history file to complete a project completion report.

The report should contain recommendations for improvement to the risk/project management, estimating and approvals processes within the company.

The programme may not be terminated when the project implementation phase has been completed. With the acceptance of project completion by the customer, the programme may move into an operation and support mode. However, the project team is usually disbanded at this point, at least to a large degree, and so a project completion report is required.

The project or programme manager for the operation and support phase of the project life-cycle is concerned with the warranty, maintenance, modification and support of the operation of the systems and/or products which result from the project phase.

The above activities may be the result of separate contracts, or an amendment to the original contract, or be a continuation of the original contract. In the case of the development of consumer goods, the mode of production may jump to the opposite end of the spectrum of production and operation's environments, and the transfer of products to consumers be achieved through lengthy and complex distribution channels. However, even here the design teams for subsequent projects have much to gain from users views, and so a feed-back loop for whole life information is needed, even though the tenure of the work has changed.

Both change control and configuration control are an essential element of reducing risk during in-service support operations. Unless a formal procedure is in place, the customer may change equipment or interfaces to his system without notice to the company, creating problems when spares or servicing are needed. Documentation will quickly become obsolete and operating instructions could become a health and safety risk.

The *RISKMAN* methodology requires that risk management is implemented throughout the project's whole life-cycle. This requires that all of the work in the above activities be evaluated for risks in achieving the project objectives.

The risk review team will normally be disbanded at the end of the major implementation phase and future reviews will be the responsibility of the programme and support managers. The contingency budgets for each of the activities will act as the control mechanism with reports being progressed as previously described.

A whole through-life support period may cover many years or even decades on some products. This is a very long *timescale* and risks will change as the products and systems approach the end of their lives. Project risk audits cannot wait to the end of the project life and must therefore be implemented at regular intervals.

As each activity is approached it is essential that the risks are evaluated at that time. Many of the activities in a support role are not pre-programmed and require response times that do not allow the full risk process to be implemented. They are small or minor projects and must be treated as such.

When major modifications (updates) are to be implemented the risks in the activity can be evaluated in the normal manner as time will generally be available to enter a risk assessment and evaluation process.

The final activity in the product/project life-cycle is product disposal. On a major project for example, a nuclear submarine, disposal becomes a major risk and if the arrangements for disposal have not been made within the original contract then the risk may have been left for the customer to face.

Disposal risks can therefore be environmental in nature or they may be market oriented in nature, such as the taking back of out-dated naval vessels with a view to selling-on to other navies in order to win the contract for their replacement. They may just be the risks involved in re-working with materials that have been re-classified as hazardous under the regulations in force, or they may just be the risks in stripping out and refurbishing an area ready for a new activity.

Risks associated with a project may therefore not stop until the contract or product is terminated in its entirety.

5.7 Summary

Risk-driven project management is the management of a project with more emphasis on the uncertainties and contingency plans that may be required, and detailed attention to the main plan when and where things go wrong. When the main plan is being achieved smoothly, little attention is required. It is, or can be, a whole-life risk management activity. The process does not require the project manager to relinquish control of the project to a risk manager, though in a major project a risk manager may be required to assist the project manager. The emphasis change is in the stricter control of the risks and the use of foresight to seek out and then manage the uncertainties.

The existing project management procedures remain totally valid. Implementing *RISKMAN* means adding to them rather than replacing them. Areas that may need adjustment are primarily in the reporting and assessments of risks.

RISKMAN encourages the selection and introduction of risk management according to the needs of the company and its projects, ranging from a basic application through an intermediate level to a comprehensive level. Existing management procedures such as change and configuration control, project status reporting, quality assurance, are little changed by application of the *RISKMAN* methodology. In many cases the emphasis is on a more strict application of these procedures, or in the case of reporting, a more stringent attention to financial status.

Management of the risk contingency budget and strict control of the spend of contingency money should lead to the benefits of risk management being achieved on the project. This will result in both increased confidence in the profitability of project activity, and a real increase in the size of that profitability.

Risk audits are essential to ensure that projects are under control and that risk management techniques are being applied.

6
Implementing *RISKMAN* Within Your Company

Every *RISKMAN* implementation in a company needs a preliminary stage of adaptation of the concepts to the company's own context. This should reflect both the level of risk management desirable and appropriate to the company's business and the maturity in risk management experience of staff who must implement any new procedures.

The risk classes, first of all, may need modification or different definitions. In each company different risk classes may be more important than others. In these cases, it may be necessary to make some modification. Some classes may need to be broken down into several, others may be able to be merged.

The customisation process depends on the actual organisation, existing responsibilities, habits and procedures, and the project problems to be faced.

Of course, implementing the method will cause some changes, but its main purpose is not to change the existing organisation, but to improve the management of it by dealing with the extra information generated by risk management.

Existing good project management practices and standards are also to be taken into account. Here again, *RISKMAN* is to be tailored to complement what is in place, wherever possible.

Finally, after tuning these parameters, an appropriate plan must be prepared to enable the methods to be introduced within the company to cover: trials, training, prototypes, wide-range use, improvement and change mechanisms. The cost of risk management must also be built-in to actual management figures.

This chapter provides keys to the implementation of the method taking account of the above-mentioned criteria.

6.1 Assessing the appropriate *RISKMAN* level

We have seen that *RISKMAN* levels are mainly targeted to fit the requirements of the projects, the readiness of the organisation to implement the techniques and the desires of the customer. The levels to be applied will have implications for the investment level a company has to make for risk management.

This financial effort is made according to overall objectives:

- improving the company's image as seen by its customers;
- enhancing its maturity in driving projects;
- making more profit.

But this requires capabilities:

- a minimal project management background;
- a motivation;
- appropriate funding and business objectives.

Figure 6.1 identifies criteria that may be used to determine the level of application of risk management that will best suit a company's capabilities.

RISKMAN application levels	Company capability and protection need				
	Project management capability required	Risk management experience	Management attitude to acceptance of risks	Risk financial exposure	Customer attitude
Basic *RISKMAN* Identifying Qualifying risk Mitigation	Minimal project management exposure	Low	Risk adverse	Low financial exposure	Minimal to medium requirement for risk management
Intermediate *RISKMAN* Basic + Quantitative Assessment Prioritising Budget assessment	Good project management	Limited	Minimal risk-taking	Medium financial exposure	Medium to high level of risk management requirement
Comprehensive *RISKMAN* Intermediate + Modelling Decision analysis Systematic Technique	Experienced project management	High	High risk-taking	High Financial exposure	High level of risk management requirement

Figure 6.1 *RISKMAN* level assessment

A company may decide that it needs several levels of *RISKMAN*, particularly if its departments (divisions) are doing business that are very different in nature. Moreover, a department is not committed to a single level of *RISKMAN* all the time. The *RISKMAN* level is an average level for operations. For simple projects, one can decide to apply a lower level. On the other hand, for more complex operations than usual, an upper level may be necessary. In this latter case, expertise and assistance from outside may also be required.

6.2 Customisation for the business

To be efficient, a risk management method must be adapted in order to be as close as possible to the way the people in the company do business every day. Therefore, it implies tailoring of the method, and also changes to some management procedures:

- Attempting to do risk identification on the basis of a standard database collated from outside is wishful thinking. Such a database can only be used as a basis on which to build one's own database.

- Applying pre-specified practices for risk mitigation can be a good starting point. Incorporating the experience of the company's best experts from such a starting point is much better.

- Adding risk management to the existing procedures or management practices is useless if both are not made complementary.

- There is little use in spending effort to quantify a risk budget if resources and skills are not in place to manage it.

The first exercise is to characterise what types of business the company is doing, and how it has organised itself to meet the business' needs. It might be necessary to introduce several levels of implementations of the *RISKMAN* if different types of business are being managed.

Changing viewpoints for projects: being a purchaser or a prime contractor leads to different types of analysis, even if some aspects are common. For example, a prime contractor would have a purchaser point of view when subcontracting. The purchaser tends to focus on particular aspects of the project: defining the need properly, selecting the right prime contractor, and on the deployment, set to work and operation phases. During the contract's realisation, the accent would be on the need for evolution control, progress and quality control. A prime contractor will focus on understanding the need and identifying an architecture of which he will ensure manufacture.

Sub-contractors on the other hand, view the project only from the aspect of their own sub-system. When the sub-contract is let, the risks associated with acquiring funding, and product definition have all been overcome, so everyone gets down to facing the risks associated with delivery deadlines, resources and technical problems. At an earlier stage in the process however, the sub-contractor may have been required to provide a quotation as part of the prime contractor's bid submission, and, at such a point the sub-contractors will have been sharing the desire of the prime contractor to win the contract. At this earlier stage he may have been concerned with political and commercial risks of a very different nature from his later areas of concern.

Teams managing internal projects, and work package managers clearly view risks from yet another perspective, and likewise their view point change as the project moves through its life cycle.

The type of business: Figure 6.2 identifies a range of industrial activities from running a process (oil refinery) to single-unit development for a single customer. This has a major impact on:

- the risk classes: the marketing class is different according to the way the company establishes its relations with customers. Making a product for a market, and delivery of a one-off are different problems. For example, such topics as contractual or financial aspects will not be handled in the same way.

- the focus on life-cycle phases is also different in terms of risks: stock management, process installation reliability are subjects of less interest for one-off projects.

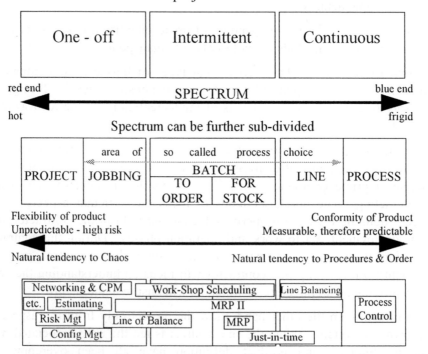

Figure 6.2 Project management in context

- the market: each market has its aspects, codes, traditions, and habits. The market assessment must support the evaluation method by providing efficient information. If this is not done, this lack of adaptation would lead to inefficient risk management resulting in effort being spent on useless analysis, and omission of important points.

- the internal organisation: will lead to process identification. The same approach may be found in other companies. However one must take into account the specific rules or traditions of a company. Several functions may be performed in one department or one function delegated into several departments, etc. The rule is to have a clear responsibility for each process.

6.3 Implementation strategy

As described earlier in this book, risk management requires changes in an organisation. It will affect the way every-day business activity is performed, encourage a new open management style and change attitudes. Therefore, implementing a method like *RISKMAN* must be directed according to a prepared strategy in order to minimise the potential negative impacts that any important change is likely to generate.

```
┌──────────────────────────────────────────────────┐
│   • Creation of an implementation team           │
│   • Definition of objectives and plan            │
│   • Identification of pilot projects             │
└──────────────────────────────────────────────────┘
                         ⇓
┌──────────────────────────────────────────────────┐
│   • Implementation team training                 │
│   • Current procedures modification              │
│   • Project team training                        │
└──────────────────────────────────────────────────┘
                         ⇓
┌──────────────────────────────────────────────────┐
│   • Pilot projects trials                        │
│   • Implement changes due to lessons learned     │
│   • Internal training                            │
└──────────────────────────────────────────────────┘
                         ⇓
┌──────────────────────────────────────────────────┐
│   • Implementation team members become the       │
│     experts in risk management                   │
│   • Extensive training                           │
└──────────────────────────────────────────────────┘
```

Figure 6.3 *RISKMAN* **Implementation steps**

The approach that we recommend is a progressive one. The purpose is to try the method on volunteer pilot projects, learn the lessons, then generalise the method. The steps in implementing *RISKMAN* are as shown in Figure 6.3.

The implementation team is made up of volunteer personnel from high level management, pilot project staff and a representative from the quality department. Some external experts may be invited. The team is in charge of the implementation operation until the end of the pilot project trials. Some of its members become the internal risk experts, and will supervise the evolution of the method as a quality progress group, where relevant, according to ISO9000 (the method is designed to be developed within the quality management system).

6.4 Detailed tailoring activities

The method has to be interfaced with a certain number of company topics. The following checklist identifies a typical set of activities:

- Identify classes, processes and typical techniques (as described in Section 6.1).

- Set a first version of the risk management database documentation:

    risk identification checklists or cause/effect diagrams;

    risk quantification guidelines and techniques;

    guidelines on risk reduction.

- Provide coherence with the internal project management standards and practices:

    definition of a risk-driven project management process;

    existing procedures modification or new procedures introduction;

    estimation process revisited;

    new reporting rules.

- Adapt the budgeting process:

    links with company analytical accounting;

    new budget allocation and release rules.

- Provide coherence with the quality system:

    existing standards and procedures.

- Explain and train to the new management rules.

6.5 Potential hurdles in implementation

Introducing risk management in an organisation will undoubtedly lead to several problems that need to be anticipated in order not to provoke method rejections. As major examples:

- shooting the messenger;
- everything is a risk;
- resistance to change;
- bad quantification;
- risk budget equivalent to the project budget.

The implementation team has an important role in sorting out these potential problems by providing expertise and anticipating the pockets of resistance. They should be able to identify appropriate approaches to win them over (authority, persuasion, involvement). In other words, a risk mitigation strategy.

7
Benefits and Conclusions

7.1 The benefits of risk management

During the course of this introduction to the *RISKMAN* project risk management methodology, many benefits have been discussed. Experience in using *RISKMAN* on projects will demonstrate a broad spread of other benefits.

Strategic benefits

- Corporate decision making is improved through the high visibility of risk exposure and also risk opportunity, both for individual major projects, and across the whole of the company's project portfolio.

- A progressive management style and a culture of continuous improvement is enhanced by the encouragement of openness in relation to risk, enabling full use of the combined expertise of the staff.

- The company's image in the eyes of clients, partners, suppliers and competitors is enhanced through the visible and highly professional approach to the crucial subject of risk.

- Ensures that threats to cost, time and performance are managed with the clear aim of meeting the company's and customer's objectives.

- Creates an awareness of the risks in making business decisions at all levels in the company.

Financial benefits

- Provides financial benefit to the organisation through improved profit potential.

- Improves management of project finance, thereby benefiting cash flow.

- Provides visibility and strict management of risk contingency.

Marketing benefits

- Improves likelihood of winning additional business.

- Improves understanding of the project through the identification of risks and proper consideration of mitigation strategies.

- Creates an understanding of the relationship between risks, cost, programme timescales and price.

- Creates an environment for the conscious acceptance of business risks on an informed basis.

- Reduces the likelihood of over-pricing by giving confidence that all risk elements have been addressed.

- Assists in the establishment of criteria for the inclusion of risk contingency and the boundaries within which negotiators can negotiate the price.

- Reduces the need for subsidies to be hidden within individual elements of the cost estimate.

Tactical or management benefits

- Ensures 'ownership' of both risks and their causes, so that they are effectively monitored, and pro-actively managed.

- Provides management with clear visibility of the risk and actions being taken to resolve them.

- Makes the relative importance of each risk immediately apparent.

- Improves contingency plans.

- Enables decision-making to be more systematic and less subjective.

- Reduces the need for time or cost escalation.

- Reduces product performance shortfalls.

- Brings realism into consideration of the trade-offs between performance, cost and time.

- Allows comparison of the robustness of projects to specific uncertainties.

- Assists in creating a 'no surprises' environment.

- Enforces selection of options only after consideration of the fall-back positions.

- Emphasises to project teams the importance of clear criteria for performance measurement.

- Provides a framework for encouraging lateral thinking in searching for better ways to mitigate risks.

- Creates an open and candid approach to risks, that encourages the staff to assist in overcoming them.

- Encourages a considered and decisive style of management, resulting in proper handling of the risks themselves, rather than the management of crisis.

- Filters and prioritises risks so that management may have clear visibility of the important risks.

- Provides for acceptance and approval of risks at the correct management level.

- Creates an awareness in all personnel of the cost implications of their actions.

7.2 Conclusions

The attitude with which project risk management is approached is crucial to its success. A common reaction to the mention of methodologies is that they discourage entrepreneurial spirit and impose a bureaucratic, mechanistic process that is lacking in interest.

The *RISKMAN* project risk management methodology dispels the above myth by providing a disciplined strategy for implementing project risk management, that creates an open-minded approach to the identification of risks. The methodology encourages risk owners to make use of lateral thinking in their search for ways to mitigate risks and inspires a calm, decisive style of management. This results in proper handling of the risks, rather than the management of crisis.

Sponsored in Europe under a Eureka initiative, *RISKMAN* has been developed to be compatible with international standards and is suitable for adoption across a wide range of industries and countries. Whilst *RISKMAN* has not been developed to provide a project risk management standard as such, companies that adopt it can use the *RISKMAN* badge to provide their customers with evidence that they have positioned themselves to manage risky projects successfully.

RISKMAN provides procedural framework guidelines that can be used across all projects, irrespective of size or complexity and that can be adapted to meet the specific project management requirements of organisations and their customers.

RISKMAN provides customers with visibility of the organisation's project management capability and methods. Prime contractors can select, with confidence, those subcontractors that have adopted the *RISKMAN* methodology, because their capability and tools to manage risks will be clearly evident.

No method can guarantee that all risks will be identified; there will always be the occasional, unexpected event which no one has predicted. A disciplined approach ensures that risks are identified objectively and that when unidentified risks (residual risks) arise, a project management framework, formed from experience, is in place to objectively assess and manage the new risks.

RISKMAN enforces a more rigorous approach to the identification and assessment of business and project risks. Realism is brought into consideration of the trade-offs, and selection of alternate mitigation strategies.

Corporate communications are improved and experience is retained, by documenting the reasons behind decisions and improved involvement of management at all levels in the project risk management process. A continuous improvement ethic is established whereby professionalism of risk management continues to increase.

The use of the *RISKMAN* standard methodology for risk management demonstrates an organisation's commitment and responsible attitude towards its customer's projects. It ensures that threats to cost, time and quality will be managed to meet both the customer's and the company's objectives.

It has been shown that by using risk management techniques, improvements can be obtained in cost estimates and the likelihood of over-pricing is reduced. This is achieved by eliminating the opportunity and need for subsidises to be hidden within individual elements of a cost estimate and by providing management with criteria that enables them to accept risks. This increases the likelihood of winning bids.

RISKMAN clearly identifies the risk (contingency) within project costs that requires managing. It provides a means for monitoring and measuring the successful implementation of project risk management and demonstrates that by the acceptance of the risk exposure and management to contain the threat, benefits can accrue to the organisation. During implementation of the project, *RISKMAN* improves the management of project finances.

RISKMAN creates an awareness and increases the understanding of the risks that arise in making business decisions, as well as emphasising the need for adequate intelligence gathering and analysis on the market and competition. *RISKMAN* therefore creates an environment for the authorisation and acceptance of business risks on an informed basis.

Higher management are provided with clear visibility of the risks and actions being taken to resolve them. This ensures that a 'no surprises' working environment is created where functional managers can take risks, on an informed and calculated basis.

RISKMAN encourages and enforces the involvement of higher management in the project process and filters and prioritises risks so that higher management may have clear visibility of the important ones.

Risk mitigation is placed at the management level where the risk is best dealt with. Acceptance and approval of risks is placed at the level that can commit the company to projects and accept the risk exposure.

RISKMAN makes the relative importance of each risk immediately apparent by improving perception of the risks and enhancing the understanding of the effects on the project decision-taking becomes more systematic and less subjective.

In summary it is concluded that the European developed *RISKMAN* Project Risk Management Methodology for applying risk management will bring many benefits to both customers and project organisations, willing to specify and adopt the methods described.

Appendix A
RISKMAN Publications

In addition to the present introductory volume, the publication set is to be made up of a set of three manuals, presented in ring binders.

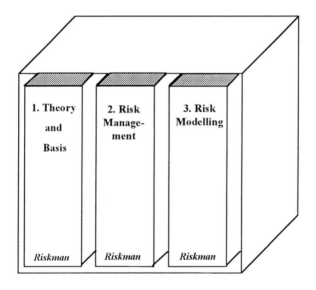

This will present a complete methodology for dealing with all aspects of project risk in an organisation. The second volume is operational and can be used directly inside the organisation.

Subsequent to the initial set, there will be a further manual published called the *RISKMAN* Implementation Guide. Everything that needs to be customised will be contained in the Implementation Guide as well as case-studies from *RISKMAN* applications. Alternative sets of *RISKMAN* sample forms will also be provided in order that the user can insert, at the relevant locations in his project management manuals, customised versions (class responsibilities, etc.). There will, therefore be no need for an organisation to develop a complete new internal procedure. Whilst tailoring will be desired by most users, the standard volumes will present the methodology in such a way as to minimise the effort and cost of such tailoring.

Appendix B
Glossary

A methodology is not a standard. Clearly *RISKMAN* can be implemented in any language and it is possible for your organisation to adopt *RISKMAN* without necessarily changing existing practice to conform with the following terminology. However, risk terms are ill-defined and variously used in the English language. It is necessary for the authors to clarify what they mean by a significant number of words and expressions to minimise misunderstanding of this text. A more exhaustive glossary will be published in the *RISKMAN* manuals, together with an explanation of any variations which may have been noticed from existing standards, guidelines and dictionaries which will include publications which have been used for reference such as:

- Norsk Standard NS5814 - Requirements for Risk Analysis
- MoD Guidelines
- CCTA Guidelines
- The Oxford English Dictionary
- Longman Guide to English Usage
- A Project Management Dictionary of Terms

Acceptance Criteria: Criteria based on regulations, standards, experience and/or theoretical evaluation that are used as a basis for acceptance of a product, project or activity.

ACWP: Actual Cost of Work Performed: *see* Earned Value.

BCWP: Budgeted Cost of Work Performed: *see* Earned Value.

BCWS: Budgeted Cost of Work Scheduled: *see* Earned Value.

Bills of Quantities: calculations for project costing as done prior to the use of the WBS, and still widely used especially in the construction industry.

BOM: Bill of Materials: *see* Product Breakdown Structure.

BS5750: British Standard for quality management, identical to the International standard ISO9000.

CCTA: The UK government agency responsible for procurement of comunications and computer systems.

CPA: Critical Path Analysis.

C/SCSC: Cost/Schedule Control Systems Criteria: a set of requirements for project management published by the US Department of Defense to ensure proper reporting by contractors on large or critical defence contracts.

Category (of risk): RISKMAN prescribes three types of risk (categories 1, 2 and 3) dependent on the way that the risks can be quantified and modelled.

Chance: uncertainty; an uncertain happening (*see* probability).

Change Control Board (CCB): board commissioned to analyse all major change requests on the system and/or project environment (modification of the technical baseline), and accept, reject or postpone them. The members of this board are usually selected from amongst the prime contractor project team and the subcontractor's project teams, and may include customer representatives.

Change Control Procedure: a method of initiating, investigating, costing and sanctioning changes to the baseline configuration and the contracted commitment, and ensuring their embodiment in the project or product.

Class (of risk): *RISKMAN* provides a list of twelve classes of risk, (*see* Diagram 2.6).

Classification of Risks: a process which assists in allocating responsibility for risks and identifying causes and potential control mechanisms.

Client: meaning also customer, principal, owner, promoter, or purchaser (*see* user).

Command failure: failure of a system due to incorrect commands or signals from the operator, or from other components.

Concern, area of concern (also qualm, apprehension or worry): used in the sense of an anxiety rather than a business. A concern will indicate a problem expressed as arising from a lack of information on skills, resources, equipment and facilities that may turn into a risk if neglected. Concerns will often resolve themselves as the infrastructure and facilities requirements are put in place.

Configuration Management: a technique to ensure that the customer actually gets what he wants.

Consequential prejudice: business costs incurred by the user in the case of a system failure - late deliveries on current contracts, late future contracts, additional financial expenses because of late payments, etc.

CTR: Cost Time and Resource: planning method for large projects developed primarily in the oil industry in the 1970s.

Decision Trees: a diagrammatic representation of a set of possible alternatives in the form of an open network that shows the alternative paths available to a decision maker. When combined with estimates of probability for the factors (cost, resources, etc.) being considered, it enables the cumulative probability of the outcomes to be calculated.

Definition baseline: set of documents, information, elements describing the system, its missions functions and performance, as well as the major milestones of its realisation, and the organisation and legal environment which are requested to achieve this. Any change on these documents modifies the scope of the project and requires approval of the purchaser and contractor.

Direct prejudice: direct costs incurred by the user in the case of a failure of a system - human and/or physical damage, repair costs, setting back to work, last work hours, etc.

Earned Value: a measure, used in the technique of Earned Value Performance Monitoring, for project progress measurement. The work actually completed is valued at the rate built in to the contract price (hence the *earned value*) as a metric to assess both cost and schedule performance throughout project execution. The main measures are Actual Cost of Work Performed (ACWP), Budgeted Cost of Work Performed (BCWP), and Budgeted Cost of Work Scheduled (BCWS).

ENF: Expected number of failures.

Evolution Control Board (ECB): the equivalent of the Change Control Board (qv), but for those projects which are in-house research or product development activities, and where there is no 'customer' and no 'contract'.

Evolution guarantee: given that a team is available to adapt the system to new requirements.

Execution period: contractual period during which the system (or part of it) is under realisation, prior to final delivery.

Functional Breakdown Structure (FBS): a hierarchical structure relating the functions of a product or service, used in value analysis techniques.

Gambling: Risk-Taking.

ISO 9000: *see* BS5750.

ITT: Invitation to Tender. Similar to RFP (Request for Proposal), and RFQ (Request for Quotation).

Impact: (in the context of risk) an estimate of the effect that the risk will have in relation to timescale, costs, product quality, safety and performance.

Inaccuracy Allowance: an allocation of time and/or money to cover uncertainties due to inaccuracy in deterministic estimates.

Indirect prejudice: indirect costs resulting from a failure of product or failure to meet contractual commitments, such as loss of market share for the user's company. Can be calculated by average growth compared to reduced growth due to loss of production capability. Generally not covered by insurance policy.

Insurance: paying a premium to some person or organisation to cover some or all of the cost of an impact, and should be indulged in when the impact is likely to be greater than the cost one anticipates being able to afford at that time.

Jobbing shop: a facility (factory etc) able to perform a series of similar projects, such as a dockyard, a steelwork fabricator, a software house, or even a hospital.

Levels of Approval: management level at which approvals are given.

Liability period: period during which the prime or subcontractor is liable for a failure of a system he has delivered.

Likelihood: *see* probability. This may be expressed on a scale of 0-1 or 0-100%.

MTBF: mean time between failure.

MTTF: mean time to fail.

Maintenance guarantee: given that a team is available to maintain.

Major Risk: a risk that has a high or medium likelihood of occurring with a significant adverse impact on the affected item(s).

Major Risk Summary: a summary statement of each major risk element, its effect, ownership and recommendations for mitigation.

Major Risk-sharing Team Member: a subcontractor who has entered into an agreement to accept a level of risk exposure greater than the risks directly associated with the subcontracted activity.

Mitigation: action to reduce, eliminate or avert the impact or probability of the risk. In many cases, it is a futuristic plan of action.

OBS: *see* Organisation Breakdown Structure

Organisation Breakdown Structure: a hierarchical structure representing the organisation by department from the Managing Director (or equivalent), through each department head, down to the individuals who constitute the human resource of the organisation.

PBS: *see* Product Breakdown Structure

PERT (Project Evaluation and Review Technique): a specific variant of CPA which uses statistical approximations to account for uncertainty in estimating. NOTE: in some texts, this term is used loosely to cover any use of critical path techniques in the planning and control of a project.

Primary failure: failure of a system due to the excessive age, bad design, bad realisation or improper installation of a component.

Prime Contractor: a company managerially, commercially and technically capable of accepting the contract from the customer, taking responsibility for co-ordinating the activities of a number of sub-system contractors, integrating their deliverables, and managing the risks to meet the customer's requirements in terms of performance, cost and timescale.

PRINCE: a project management method developed for infprmation technology projects under the auspices of the CCTA (qv), and published by NCC Blackwell.

Probability: the likelihood (chance) that an event will occur measured on a scale of 0-1 (0 indicating cannot occur and 1 indicating certain to occur). Probability is a statistical term. The term *likelihood* is preferred.

Product Breakdown Structure: a hierarchical structure which breaks down the product itself into constituent parts, in a similar way to a Bill of Materials. Should be closely related to the Drawing Register or the System Architecture in many development environments.

Project Business Case: the business case that is prepared to support the requirement for a significant investment in a single project which may be in areas such as marketing, research, development, proposal preparations, acquisitions or joint ventures.

Project Finance: the funding required to implement the project in its totality. Such funding may be from internal sources or external sources, the cost of such funding being a direct project cost.

Project Risk Manager: a person assigned to a project to be responsible for the production and management of the risk plan.

Qualitative Risk Assessment: a description of the risk, likelihood of the risk occurring, its impact, statements of how the risk impact may be contained, what fallback/recovery measurers are available, and who owns the risk (*see* Risk Estimating).

Quality Management: control of quality. Initially applied to the product, now applied to the management process for the whole company. Total Quality Management (TQM) is an extension of the concept, focusing on customer orientation.

Quantitative Risk Assessment: the analysis of risk estimates to establish the project schedule costs/forecast using probabilistic data and other identified uncertainties to determine the spread of likely outcomes.

Reliability: the duration or probability of failure-free performance under stated conditions; the probability that a product will perform its intended function for a specified period of time under stated conditions.

Risk: a function of both the likelihood (probability) of an event (usually, but not necessarily, an adverse event) occurring, and its impact. The impact may manifest itself in financial loss or gain, time delay or schedule improvement, reduction or increase in product performance and/or acceptability.

Risk Impact: *see* Impact.

Risk-taking: should be deliberate when the likely or possible outcome is considered desirable in comparison with the likely cost, one should take the risk. Risk-taking is endemic in all business activity, and is more prevalent in everyday living than most people recognise.

Risk Allowance: an allocation of time and/or money to cover uncertainties due to inaccuracy in deterministic estimates and/or the occurrence of risk events.

Risk Allowance = Σ (inaccuracy allowances + uncertainty allowances)

Risk Analysis: the work involved in identifying and evaluating risks.

Risk Appraisal: the work involved in identifying and assessing, and mitigation planning of risks.

Risk Budget: allocation of cost and schedule allowance held in reserve to be spent only with the emergence of uncertainties (risks).

Risk Category: *see* Category.

Risk Class: *see* Class.

Risk Consequences: the immediate effect of a risk occurring and the follow-on effect on other indirectly associated activities. Consequences of risks must be followed through to the end of their effect, which can then always be measured in financial terms.

Risk Contingency: the financial and schedule cost estimate that is included in the price build-up and schedule commitment to take account of the mitigation action and uncertainty remaining with a programme.

Risk Database: a database that contains the records of all risks associated with a project.

Risk Description: a unique description of the risk element that clearly identified and defines the boundaries of the risk.

Risk Estimating: quantifying the impact and likelihood of a risk.

Risk Evaluation: the process of determining the significance or value of the risk element, based on evaluation of the probability of occurrence and estimated impact of the adverse event(s) on the activity being evaluated.

Risk Exposure: defined as the product of the financial impact value and its probability of occurrence.

Risk Factor (RF): the mathematical interaction of Probability (likelihood) (P) and Impact (I) on a scale of 0-1, given by $(RF) = P + I - P * I$.

Risk Management: the complete process involved in identifying risks, and assessing them for likelihood and potential impact. This includes the development of suitable strategies to mitigate the impacts and the activities involved in budgeting for risk, controlling and reporting risk status, and the management of the risks until consequences are fully resolved.

Risk Management Plan: a formal plan which may be a sub-set of the project management plan, which describes how risks will be managed throughout the life of the project. It covers such issues as responsibility for risks, risk budget, methods, resources, reporting, monitoring, etc.

Risk Management Strategy: a formal statement of the strategy to be adopted throughout the life of a project that states how risk management is to be implemented, levels of resources to be used, balance between intramural and extramural resources, and roles of subcontractors.

Risk Model: a tool version of the project programme that enables prediction of the spread of exposure within the programme's duration, milestones, deliverables and costs. It is effectively an extension of a project's deterministic programme, containing all the estimates of uncertainties for costs, timescale and resource, as well as factors that create perturbation (e.g. weather), and mathematical expressions (algorithms) (e.g. Dempster/Shafer, Monte Carlo, Latin Hypercube and Bayesian) that enables random sampling of the risk to be implemented, and the range of exposure estimated. The latter often involves computing a large number of calculations.

Risk Portfolio: hard copy of all risk data, usually in the form of completed forms or printed from a computerised risk support system.

Risk Prioritising: the process involved in filtering, grouping and placing in order of priority, the risks following assessment.

Risk Register: the printed output of risks contained in a database.

Risk Summary: is a summary of each risk element, its effect, ownership and recommendations for mitigation.

Risk Trigger: an event which can be identified and indicates that risks need to be re-assessed and/or mitigation action initiated to reduce the risk to an acceptable level.

Risk Type: *see* Type.

Rolling wave: a concept of planning in which the complete plan is maintained only at a high level (ie: not very detailed), and portions or stages are broken down into much more detail only at the time that it becomes necessary in order to control that phase.

Sanction: the decision to authorise investment in a business or project, or to take a specific course of action.

Scope of Work: a precise definition of the work involved in a work package (*see* Work Breakdown Structure).

Secondary failure: failure of a system due to the use of a component in excessive conditions, i.e. heat, vibration.

Sensitivity Analysis: determining the stability of a project plan and the susceptibility of the project outcome to change as a result of risk occurrences or uncertainty in estimates. Sensitivity can be tested by assessing the effect on the outcome of a project or activity by changing one or more of the risk variables.

Taxonomy: *see* Classification of Risks.

Technical baseline: set of documents, information, components, sub-systems describing the system, its design, realisation, production and test strategy, as well as the detailed description of its realisation plan (schedules, resources). Everything in the technical baseline is made in compliance with the definition baseline and, if not, has proper authorisation.

Three-point Estimating: allowing for uncertainty in estimates by defining the distribution of possible task durations by the provision of three duration estimates: the minimum, maximum and target durations. This approach is used in all network-based risk scheduling processes.

TickIT a special version of BS5750 (qv) tailored for Information Technology systems development

Tolerances: the range of values above and below the estimated project cost, duration or performance within which the final value is likely to fall.

Top-down/Bottom-up: in project management, the philosophy of transforming rough-cut estimates into detailed plans using Work Breakdown Structures, and then maintaining the WBS as the primary means of controlling the project. Overall project progress is determined by summarisation up to the top level of the WBS again.

TQM: *see* Quality Management.

Type (of risk): *RISKMAN's* twelve classes of risk have been broken down into various types.

Uncertainty Allowance: an allocation of time and/or money to cover uncertainties due to the occurrence of risk events.

User: the ultimate customer.

Validity period: contractual period of time during which the contract links two parties. Generally:

validity period = execution period extended to include residual liability period.

Variation: a change to a contractor's work order under the terms of contract

WBS: *see* Work Breakdown Structure.

Work Breakdown Structure: a hierarchical coded structure which breaks down all the work in a project through various levels into work packages, which are the responsibility of one person. Each work package must have a scope of work, a budget, and a schedule, which are formally accepted by the work package manager.

Work package: identified contractual work done under certain conditions by the prime contractor or subcontractor.

Appendix C
Risk Modelling

The techniques which may be employed to address risk analysis and management may be categorised into:

- Methods which are best suited to the need to identify and classify potential risks.

- Numerical analysis methods which can be used to quantify risks and evaluate the probable impact of such risks.

- Methods which may be used to define risk reduction actions, mitigation strategies and contingency plans.

- Processes which have been designed to produce a definitive answer to questions which may be posed by specific project risk issues.

Many of these techniques were not specifically designed to address project risk analysis, but their successful application in inherently uncertain situations make them useful in analysing project risks.

Disciplines such as Operational Research and Quality Control have been the source of various modelling methods, many of which are applicable to the analysis of project risks. Unfortunately some seemingly invaluable approaches have proved to be difficult, if not impossible, to apply to project planning situations. For instance, the classical Operational Research technique of network analysis is capable of addressing both deterministic and stochastic models, but the exploitation of this technique in project planning (Critical Path Analysis) has, so far, only been successfully applied to deterministic models.

The application of statistical analysis and simulation techniques, amongst others, to deterministic network models provides a means of quantifying the uncertainty that exists in scheduling and budgeting projects, but does not adequately address other uncertain elements. For example, the question of whether or not a particular project task will need to be undertaken, depending upon preceding circumstances, is difficult to model. Providing that there is certainty, within reasonable bounds, that the task will be performed, then the uncertainty concerning the duration and expenditure which should be allowed can be adequately modelled.

The table in Figure C.1 provides a non-exhaustive list of the types of models which can be used to address specific project risk analysis issues.

Model type	Risk application	Examples
Tabular	Risk evaluation	Spreadsheets; matrices
Hierarchical	Risk identification	Work, functional, product and organisation breakdown structures
Network	Project scheduling	PERT; Monte Carlo simulation; Controlled Interval and Memory
Logic	Risk identification	Ishikawa diagrams; Markov chains
	Risk Quantification	Probability and decision trees
Mathematical	Risk quantification	Statistical analysis methods; sampling models

Figure C.1 Risk models

C.1 Qualitative prioritisation

Perhaps the most rudimentary, but far from worthless, procedure which can be employed to evaluate project risks, is that which uses a subjective assessment of the probable impact of various risks upon the project. This somewhat humble process is disguised behind the rather magniloquent title of qualitative prioritisation.

Such an approach is dependent upon the development of a comprehensive and rigorous risk taxonomy. Without a substantive taxonomy, a subjective assessment of risk will tend to become a major source of risk itself. For instance, failure to classify a risk as, say, contractual in nature; even though it may be subjectively evaluated as significant in terms of its impact upon the project; may result in a missed opportunity to mitigate the risk, perhaps to the point of elimination, by careful construction of a contractual clause.

Figure C.2 illustrates an approach to grading the qualitative prioritisation of risk.

In Figure C.2 a significance index is applied to each risk. This numerically describes its effect upon the realisation of the project, combined with the difficulty in effectively addressing the risk.

Risk description			Test facility not available		
Classification			**Programme**		
Significance Index		2	Grading		6
	Impact	Low	Medium	High	
Likelihood	Indices	1	2	3	
Low	1	1	2	⟨3⟩	
Medium	2	2	4	6	
High	3	3	6	9	

Figure C.2 Grading the qualitative prioritisation of risk

The impact, i.e. the consequential cost in terms of expenditure or time is assessed, together with the likelihood of it happening.

A specifically identified risk is graded by multiplying its significance index by the product of its likelihood and impact indices.

In the example in the figure, the unavailability of a test facility is judged to be moderately significant (2 on a scale of 1 to 5, say). The likelihood of this is assessed to be low, but the impact is perceived to be high.

The risk of a test facility being unavailable is graded 6.

When all risks have been similarly graded, they should be addressed in reverse order of their grade (perhaps using in the order of the most significant first, i.e. more systematic analytical methods).

C.2 Cause and effect analysis

That which we tend to describe as a project risk is the actual manifestation of an effect, which usually degrades the ability to realise the project's objectives. It is possible to create strategies to mitigate the effects of risk and develop contingency plans, or respond effectively, in order to address the circumstances which arise from the effects of risk. However, it may be more productive to identify the causative influences which may conspire to produce an effect, and thereby take steps to dispose of the cause and so eliminate the risk. Ishikawa diagrams or cause and effect diagrams (sometimes called fish bone diagrams), and associated analytical procedures, were developed to address quality control issues and are ideal for identifying the potential causes of project risks.

Figure C.3 shows a simple cause and effect (Ishikawa) diagram.

It is necessary to recognise that a single effect may be the result of a complex interaction of diverse causes. For example schedule delays may be caused by aspects of productivity, purchasing procedures, technical difficulty or processes. Similarly, a single cause may be a contributor, to some degree, to a variety of effects and, therefore, project risks. For example inadequate purchasing procedures may, to some degree, degrade the project schedule, inflate the cost or impair the quality of the desired product.

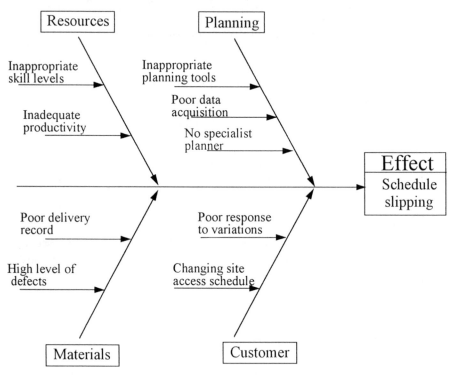

Figure C.3 Simple cause and effect (Ishikawa) Diagram

If such a model is used to identify the causative influences of a specific effect, it is important to be aware that the identified cause may, itself, be an effect of a higher level cause. It may be necessary to construct a number of Ishikawa diagrams to define the seminal cause, and this is to be preferred to attempting to construct a complex model of interactions.

Several statistical analysis methods exist to establish the relationships of cause and effect, but for most practical purposes project risk analysis can be adequately served by a subjective correlation of cause and effect. Similarly, numerical analysis models and techniques exist to quantify the probability of combinations of causes to contribute to an effect.

C.3 Simple probabilistic analysis using spreadsheets

When the probability factor of a risk is either a single value, or the result of a relatively straightforward combination (e.g. single and/or), then a spreadsheet model for probabilistic analysis may be ideal. Skill in the exploitation of computer based spreadsheet systems is prolific, and such data presentations are readily understood and accepted.

Probability factors and impact assessments of risks can be manipulated to produce *factored risk evaluations* which may then be used to provide a contribution to the risk budget. Aggregations of factored evaluations may be generated, at a variety of levels, to produce comprehensive risk evaluations.

Figure C4 shows a possible spreadsheet approach to analysing risk.

WBS code	Risk description	Impact	Prob.	And Impact	Prob.	Value
A1.01	Sub-total					£5,000
A1.01	Sub-total					3 days
A1.01.01	Incurred penalties	£15,000	0.2			£3,000
A1.01.02	Re-test MCS	£ 2,000	0.4	£1,000	0.5	£1,300
A1.01.02	Re-test MCS	2 weeks	0.4	1 week	0.2	5 days
A1.01.03	Replace loops	£ 5,000	0.4	£2,000	0.5	£3,000

Figure C.4 Simple spreadsheet for risk analysis

C.4 Probability and decision trees

C.4.1 Probability

Whilst risk may be frequently assessed from an instinctive basis, there are occasions when a more systematic approach will produce a more objective quantification. Numerical methods may provide an appropriate mathematical model which will produce a viable solution. If the creation of such a model is particularly difficult, or even inappropriate, then it may be more effective to employ a logical model with base data to produce the desired result.

There are a number of suitable modelling methods but perhaps the most practical is the construction of a probability tree. A decision tree is a particular application of probability trees.

A logical sequence of chance events is defined and the number of branches identifies all the potential conclusions from a combination of uncertain situations. The probabilities of all the outcomes of a chance event are applied to the tree and the combinations can be identified and calculated.

The approach is best illustrated by describing an example. Let's say that a number of items are to be used on a product and there is statistical evidence to suppose that 2% of them will be actually defective on receipt. Quality tests are only 95% effective. In other words, 5% of the non-defective items will be incorrectly rejected by the quality test and 5% of those which are defective will be accepted. It is, of course, possible to describe the combinations of these probabilities in terms of fairly simple mathematical models, but for the purposes of illustration a probability tree is chosen.

The logical sequence of this situation is shown in Figure C.5 which has four possible outcomes:

(1) Non-defective items rejected by the test.

(2) Non-defective items accepted by the test.

(3) Defective items rejected by the test.

(4) Defective items accepted by the test.

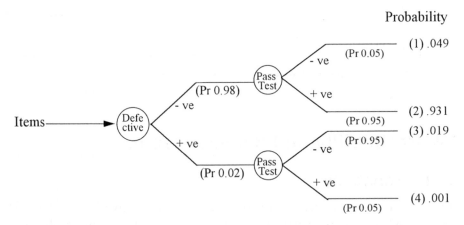

Figure C.5 Probability tree

The probability of each outcome can be calculated by multiplying the individual values along a sequence. This would give:

Pr(1) = 0.049; Pr(2) = 0.931; Pr(3) 0.019; Pr(4) = 0.001

Such results can then be used in a spreadsheet, together with assessments of the consequences, in terms of both schedule and cost, to produce a probabilistic analysis.

C.4.2 Decision trees

A probability tree is defined in terms of uncertain events. The same approach can be used to indicate an appropriate action, or desired choice. Decision nodes, together with all possible outcomes, can be included in sequences of uncertain events. Specific outcomes are of course certainties, in other words the probability of a decision is 1.0.

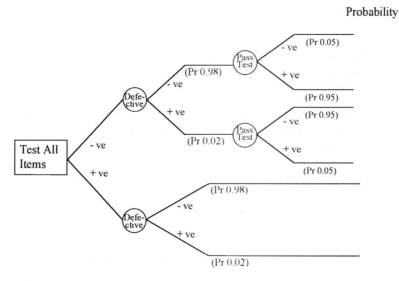

Figure C.6 Decision Tree

In the previous example a decision could be included which made the choice between testing items, or not. The resultant diagram is shown in Figure C.6 and produces two additional outcomes:

(5)   Untested non-defective items with Pr = 0.98

(6)   Untested defective items with Pr = 0.02

If it was determined that the consequential cost of rejecting non-defective items was £10000, and that of accepting defective items was £50,000, the decision could be evaluated as:

Expected consequential cost of testing all items = £ 540

(Pr(1) x £10,000)+(Pr(4) x £50,000) = (0.049x£10,000) + (0.001x£50,000)

Expected consequential cost of not testing all items = £1,000

Pr(6) x £50,000 = 0.02 x £50,000

It is apparent that including a test is likely to have a smaller consequence and would therefore be a better decision. But note that the risk is not eliminated by this decision, merely mitigated.

Decision trees can be useful in helping to quantify probabilities of complex combinations of chance occurrences, supporting decision making, and defining mitigation strategies and contingency plans.

C.5 Schedule risk analysis techniques

The inherent deterministic and definitive nature of Critical Path Analysis (CPA) masks the uncertainty which is intrinsic to the planning of projects.

A significant degree of faith is placed upon the technique of CPA for schedule planning. However, because of the inherently uncertain nature of the estimating process, one should be very careful not to place too much reliance upon the schedule so produced.

To illustrate this, consider a sequence of three activities produces a CPA calculated duration of 40 weeks. One could only have absolute confidence in that result if one was absolutely confident about the planned duration of each activity. If one was only, say, 80% confident in each of the planned durations, then Bayesian principles would determine that one should only be a little more than 50% confident in completing the sequence by the end of week 40!

C.5.1 PERT

The earliest attempt to address the general lack of reliability in the validity of schedules produced from network analysis, in its various forms, gave rise to the technique now known as **Programme Evaluation and Review Technique** (PERT).

Developed by Booze, Allen & Hamilton in the 1950s in support of the US Navy's Polaris missile development programme, PERT is a proven method of improving confidence in the schedules produced by CPA. All other, network based, schedule risk analysis methods and systems are derived from the principles laid down in PERT.

PERT uses a statistically derived expected duration for individual activities, based upon three estimated durations:

- An optimistic duration: The minimum time in which one would expect to complete the task.

- The most likely duration: The time in which one would normally expect to complete the task.

- The pessimistic duration: The maximum time in which one would expect to complete the task.

These estimates are used to calculate an expected duration for each activity, and an expected duration for any sequence of activities. By employing the properties of the Beta distribution, one can be definitively 50% confident in this result. The process also produces factors (variances and standard deviations) which can be used to inflate the expected duration to a value which corresponds to a required confidence level.

Whilst the schedule planning process retains its uncertain nature, the use of PERT, and other similar methods, enables the degree of uncertainty to be measured.

C.5.2 Monte Carlo

In the 1970s an increasing belief in the reliability of simulation techniques to indicate the likely outcome of, hitherto, unpredictable situations, together with almost unlimited data processing capability, led to the application of such techniques to address the uncertainty of project scheduling. This has resulted in a number of simulation based techniques, and supporting computer applications, which we categorise as Monte Carlo simulations.

The term Monte Carlo is used to describe procedures which employ randomly generated data to fuel the simulation of a defined process, to produce a realistically possible result. If the procedure is repeated many times, numerous possible results will be produced. Statistical principles can then be used to predict the likelihood of a specific outcome.

As with PERT, Monte Carlo simulation uses three estimated durations for each activity. The hypothesis, again as with PERT, is that these estimates will form the basis of a normal Beta distribution of all possible durations. CPA is performed upon the network, with times for activities being "randomly" generated to conform to each activity's distribution, (i.e. the generated duration is more likely to be closer to the most likely duration than the extremes), and a possible schedule produced. The resultant completion date is noted and the procedure repeated.

A sufficient number of repetitions will produce a range of completion dates which will tend to be normally distributed about the arithmetic mean (average) date. Statistical methods can then be used to predict the likelihood of completing the schedule by any specific date, or what time scale should be allowed to provide a specific confidence level.

A similar approach can be adopted to the forecasting of likely project costs and, providing that a reliable schedule/cost relationship is established, a comprehensive forecast of probable project out-turn can be made. Figure 2.10 shows a typical comprehensive cost and schedule probability chart which may be produced by a Monte Carlo-based system.

C.5.3 Controlled Interval and Memory

Earlier in this section it was demonstrated how a typical activity network is capable of accumulating uncertainty. PERT and Monte Carlo simulation techniques address this situation by sampling the possible solutions, thereby enabling a statistical analysis of the results. Controlled interval techniques approach the problem by exploiting the characteristic of networks to accumulate uncertainty.

The range of possible durations of a network activity is used to generate a range of start dates for any succeeding activity. This, when combined with the range of possible durations for the succeeding activity, produces a range of possible completion dates for that activity, which is then used as a range of start dates for succeeding activities, and so on through the network.

Figure C.7 illustrates this process using just a few activities.

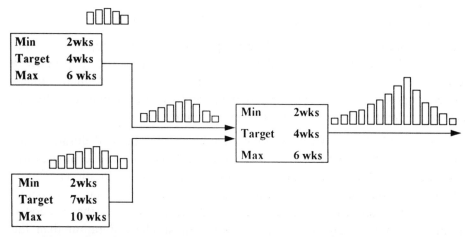

Min	2wks
Target	4wks
Max	6 wks

Min	2wks
Target	4wks
Max	6 wks

Min	2wks
Target	7wks
Max	10 wks

Figure C.7 Controlled Interval and Memory Method

This progression through the network, culminates in a potentially wide range of completion dates for those activities which terminate the project network. The minimum date of completion would be that which would derive from a schedule in which all activities were completed in their minimum expected time. The maximum date, of course, would result from a situation in which all activities took the forecast maximum amount of time. All dates between the minimum and maximum values are possible completion dates. Using the properties of a normal distribution of values it is possible to calculate the statistical probability of completing a series of activities - a project - within a specific time scale.

Because the range of possible completion dates is liable to be very large for all but the most trivial of project situations, it is advantageous to consider possible durations in terms of intervals. After all, most schedules use an interval of a day, this being considered to be a sufficiently small value for most planning purposes. The use of a day interval for controlled interval methods would produce a very large, well-defined range of results, but would require a significant computational effort. For most project situations, this may be considered to be unnecessary, and larger intervals may produce an adequately defined result. For instance, an interval of a week would suit most situations, while significantly reducing the computational effort required. Even an interval of a month may prove to be adequate.

The production of a class interval-based solution may indicate the need for a different approach to the analysis of the result. The use of the median and other positional values may be found to be more useful.

Figure C.8 shows an interval-based cumulative frequency curve, together with median and quartile values.

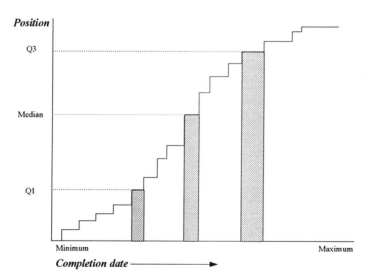

Figure C.8 Interval-based cumulative frequency curve

Appendix D
Dependability Techniques

The purpose of a dependability technique is to analyse a system's behaviour, starting at the design level, in order to identify the improvements making it more reliable. Amongst the most employed techniques we find:

Preliminary danger analysis: this consists in identifying the components of a system on one side, and the potential dangers in use of the system, on the other side. No cause-effect link is drawn between components and dangers. It is quite a simple technique and is generally used as a basis for the other techniques.

Failure modes, their effects and criticality analysis (FMECA): in this technique, the use identifies the causes of a particular failure, the component concerned, the impact of the failure, and its probability. It is a second step in dependability techniques, having one level of causes:

- Fault tree: this is a tree describing the logic combination of causes leading to a particular failure. Here the sequences of causes and effects are not limited, which enables a more precise analysis.

- Markov chains: here the system is modelled as a finite state machine, with working states and fault states. A probability is associated with the transitions between states. The system MTTF can then be evaluated.

Appendix E
Risk Quantification Techniques

In this section we present some examples of useful impact evaluation techniques. The techniques are sorted by risk class.

Class	Undesirable consequence (risk)	Techniques
Strategic	Loss of market	Impact = Gross value of market segment x (expected % - new % if risk occurs)
	Deficit	Analytical accounting General accounting

		Financial analysis:
		    cash flow analysis
		    milestones
		    actualisation

Commercial	Wasting sale effort	Total cost of:
		    commercial meetings
		    cost estimate realisation
		    preliminary studies
		    bid realisation

	Lose the customer	Total cost of:
		    unpaid work
		    unemployment
		    financial expenses
		    supplier and subcontractor
		Indirect prejudice

	Sale with a negative margin	Programme budget Risk budget Margin analysis

Class	Undesirable consequence (risk)	Techniques

Commercial (continued)	Paying penalties	Impact = D x M x R
		   D: no. of open days
		   M: cost/day/man
		   R: average resource level
		Direct or consequential
		   prejudice

Legal	Incur liabilities	Direct prejudice Consequential prejudice Indirect prejudice

	Not being paid	Total cost of:
		   unpaid works
		   unemployment
		   financial expenses
		   suppliers and subcontractors

Financial	Generate financial expenses	Cash flow analysis
		Cost of loan: B × i × t, where:
		   B: borrowed amount
		   t: time, i: interest rate
		Long-term interest rates

	Increase work without compensation	Value analysis Traceability matrix WBS, OBS, PBS Analytical accounting
	Unfavourable exchange rates	Potential new rate x financial amount to be converted
Organisation	Suppliers' overcosts	Contractor clauses

	Subcontractor's overcosts	PERT
		GANTT
		Master plan
		Monte Carlo simulation
		   Time
		   Cost

	Additional effort	

Class	Undesirable consequence (risk)	Techniques

Organisation (continued)	Additional effort	Estimation techniques
		  Heuristics
		  History
		  Regression
		  Parametric estimating
		WBS, OBS, PBS
		Extrapolation techniques
		  45° diagram
		  PUTNAM model

Programme	Manufacturing overcost	PERT Scheduling Monte Carlo simulation WBS, OBS, PBS Estimating techniques Learning curves Extrapolation techniques

	Installation locked	Costs:
		  refitting deliveries
		  maintaining the team

	Stock generation	Costs:
		  offices
		  stock maintenance
		  insurance
		  stock management

In-service	System failure leads to an accident	Human injury Direct prejudice Consequential prejudice Indirect prejudice
	Maintenance overcosts	MTTF, MTBF, MTR, MUT Intervention costs Supplies Correction costs

Appendix F
Risk Mitigation Techniques

The techniques are here presented by risk class and reduction axis. They are only examples and cannot be considered as a ready-to-use standard for a company. It is the purpose of the *RISKMAN* methodology to encourage company improvements in the field of risk reduction. Therefore this kind of material must be tailored and enhanced, based on experience.

Risk class	Reduction axes	Available techniques and additional information
External risks	Insurance	
Strategic	Information acquisition	Market analysis Scenario analysis Multi-criteria evaluation Acquisition of patents
	Cause removal	Acquisition and sales Direct grants (government funding) Indirect grants
	Share	Research of partners
Commercial	Information acquisition	Identity of decision-maker Competition User needs analysis Value analysis Cost estimate realisation
	Cause removal	No bid decision "Get out" clauses in contract Get clients to change requirements Commercial meetings Meetings with decision-makers Customer follow-up

Risk class	Reduction axes	Available techniques and additional information
Marketing	Information acquisition	Modelling Prototyping Value analysis Ergonomy studies Market analysis Investigations
Legal	Contingency	Contingency budgets Inflation clauses in contract Relative delivery dates Client duties and impact on deliveries Contingency for late delivery penalties
Contractual	Early control	Specifications validation Validation strategy definition Permanent progress control Quality plan (annexe of the contract) Development plan
	Cause removal	Negotiation Cost estimate realisation Factoring Dependability
	Share	Share risks with customer Share risks with partners and subcontractors
	Insurance	Warranty for work achievement Bank warranties International trade warranties Liability
Organisation	Contingency	Contingency planning Skills and resources management Risk budget Master plan Advanced planning techniques

Risk class	Reduction axes	Available techniques and additional information
Programme	Early control	Quality plan
		Development plan
		Configuration control
		Reporting
		E.C.B.
		C.C.B.
Technical	Information acquisition	Prototypes
		Simulation
		Value analysis
		Re-use
		Products/components acquired
		Consulting
	Cause removal	Dependability/reliability
		System design
		Adequate process
Programme	Back-up plan	Integration and installation modularity
		Acceptance strategy
		Several suppliers
		Subcontracting
		Additional effort
		Technical solutions
	Share	Suppliers and subcontractors
		Commitment on delivery date
		Commitment on specifications
		Contract management
		Subcontractor follow-up
	Insurance	Warranty for work achievement
		Life insurance for key people
		Key people commitment
Organisation	Early control	Suppliers' quality control
		Quality measures
		Productivity measures

Risk class	Reduction axes	Available techniques and additional information
Organisation	Cause removal	Ishikawa diagram
		Cause-effects diagram
		Pareto diagram
		Distribution laws
	Back-up plan	Back-up process means
		Energy supply
		Team management
		Maintenance contracts
	Insurance	Liability
		Material damages
		Material availability
		Temporary unemployment
In-service	Cause removal	Dependability
		Maintenance by anticipation
	Insurance	Warranties
	Back-up plan	Degraded modes definition
		Additional material

Index